Northern California
Curiosities

Help Us Keep This Guide Up to Date

Every effort has been made by the author and editors to make this guide as accurate and useful as possible. However, many things can change after a guide is published—establishments close, phone numbers change, hiking trails are rerouted, facilities come under new management, etc.

We would love to hear from you concerning your experiences with this guide and how you feel it could be made better and be kept up to date. While we may not be able to respond to all comments and suggestions, we'll take them to heart and we'll also make certain to share them with the author. Please send your comments and suggestions to the following address:

The Globe Pequot Press
Reader Response/Editorial Department
P.O. Box 480
Guilford, CT 06437

Or you may e-mail us at:

editorial@GlobePequot.com

Thanks for your input, and happy travels!

INSIDERS'GUIDE®

Curiosities Series

Northern California
Curiosities

Quirky Characters, Roadside Oddities & Other Offbeat Stuff

Saul Rubin

INSIDERS'GUIDE®

GUILFORD, CONNECTICUT
AN IMPRINT OF THE GLOBE PEQUOT PRESS

The prices and rates listed in this guidebook were confirmed at press time. We recommend, however, that you call establishments to obtain current information before traveling.

INSIDERS' GUIDE®

Cover photos by the author except lower left by Todd Grosser.
Interior photos by the author unless otherwise noted.
Text design by Bill Brown
Layout by Debbie Nicholais
Maps by Rusty Nelson © The Globe Pequot Press

ISSN 1555-4007
ISBN 0-7627-2899-X

Manufactured in the United States of America
First Edition/First Printing

*To Bethany and Naomi, who make life's journey
a great adventure.*

Acknowledgments

*Thanks to Al and Bea for helping out in so many ways and
to Michael for great breakfasts and help with research in
San Francisco. Love for The Club for keeping me in good
spirits. And thanks to the many Northern Californians
who shared their stories to make this book possible.*

Contents

Introduction

In the mid-nineteenth century a suddenly broke San Francisco businessman began wearing a military jacket and feathered cap and declared himself Emperor of the United States. Now in other parts of the country, a man like this would be quickly hauled off to an asylum. But that didn't happen to Joshua Norton, or as he now called himself, Norton I. No, San Franciscans embraced their emperor and his fanciful sense of reality, saluting him in the street and offering him royal perks such as free theater tickets and restaurant meals.

Emperor Norton's story is part of the San Francisco chapter of this book. More importantly, it's part of what makes Northern California, and its people, so special. This is an area with not only a high tolerance of diverse lifestyles and personalities, but a mindset that celebrates them as well. The San Francisco Bay Area sets the tone for this liberal spirit, but it reverberates throughout the region, from Santa Cruz to the south, where the university's mascot is a slimy slug, to the Mount Shasta area up north, where there are as many chanters and mystics as most places have plumbers.

People migrate here not to settle in a geographical space but to explore the far-out reaches of their minds. How else can you explain Axel Erlandson, who spent a lifetime making trees grow in contorted, fantastic shapes, a collection he displayed as the Circus Trees? His trees live on today in Gilroy, and his story is featured in the Central Coast and Valley chapter. I'm from New England, and if anyone tried to grow trees in crooked shapes there, well, I'm sure everyone would just tell him to grow them straight like they were meant to be. But Erlandson is a folk hero in California.

Even the marine life here picks up on the Northern California vibe. That's how you get the story of sea lions that have taken over a dock in a tourist area in San Francisco to stage impromptu performances for an adoring public, instead of just sitting on a big rock out at sea like their ancestors did. Then there's the story of the whale that broke away from his migratory group one year to go on an extended individual tour of San Francisco Bay.

In this book I've captured the people, places, events, and even the ghosts that reflect Northern California's offbeat nature. It goes further than the Northern California that you already know, beyond the obvious charms of San Francisco, Napa Valley, the scenic coast, and the majestic mountains. It's a journey to the edge of a place, filled with wonder and amusement. I hope you enjoy it.

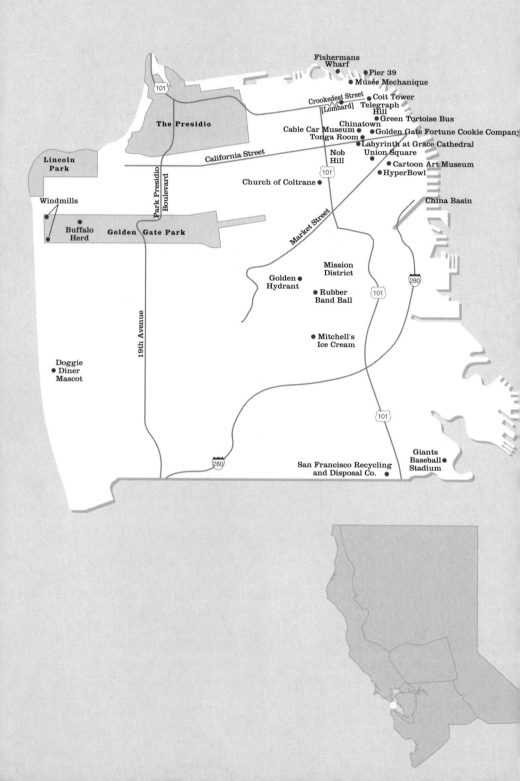

SAN FRANCISCO

Fishermans Wharf
Pier 39
Musée Mechanique
Crookedest Street
[Lombard]
Coit Tower
Telegraph Hill
Green Tortoise Bus
Chinatown
Cable Car Museum
Golden Gate Fortune Cookie Company
Tonga Room
Labyrinth at Grace Cathedral
Nob Hill
Union Square
Cartoon Art Museum
HyperBowl
Church of Coltrane
China Basin

The Presidio

Lincoln Park

California Street

Park Presidio Boulevard

Windmills
Buffalo Herd
Golden Gate Park

Market Street

Mission District
Golden Hydrant
Rubber Band Ball

19th Avenue

Mitchell's Ice Cream

Doggie Diner Mascot

Giants Baseball Stadium

San Francisco Recycling and Disposal Co.

San Francisco

A RACE THAT'S WAY OFF COURSE

Thousands of people spend hours getting in the right condition to run in the annual Bay to Breakers race. To some that means drinking plenty of beer, or perhaps something Polynesian with rum. To others it's designing an improbable costume more appropriate for Mardi Gras than a foot race. It doesn't matter because most entrants aren't trying to win. Their primary goal is to look fabulous as they cross the starting line. There's not a care about how they'll fare at the finish, or whether they'll even get there.

The Bay to Breakers is a moving carnival in sneakers. It's also the world's biggest road race, setting a record with 102,500 runners in 1986.

Some people who enter actually care about winning the race. These racers prepare by practicing their running, training that would never occur to the majority of the field. The elite crowd speeds along the course, which starts downtown and ends at the ocean along the Great Highway, and finishes in about thirty-five minutes. Meanwhile many runners are still at the start, bunched up with thousands of others. In some years it takes up to ninety minutes for everyone just to cross the starting point.

And what a sight it is—thousands of people outfitted in outlandish costumes. There are people dressed as everything from vegetables to San Francisco landmarks. There's a team of spawning salmon who run backwards while wearing fish outfits. One year a man came dressed in drag while carting two small Victorian houses behind him. Lots of people wear bathrobes to this morning competition. Some women jog along in full wedding regalia. To others, clothing is optional. A growing number of people opt to run naked, a tradition known as the Bare to Breakers.

Victory for most folks is not how fast they get to the finish but how many times along the way they're asked to stop and pose for pictures.

The race, held each May, began in 1912 as part of efforts to boost community spirit after the 1906 earthquake. It was run as a conventional race for decades until costumed runners begin lacing up to join in the 1970s. Things have pretty much gotten out of hand since.

A DOGGED PRESERVATION EFFORT

The dog had his day all right, but it wasn't a very good one. Disastrous, in fact. The 7-foot-tall fiberglass dachshund, a mascot for a once-popular chain of hot dog stands known as Doggie Diners, had tumbled from atop a pole during a windstorm and landed on its pointy schnoz. The literal nosedive occurred April 1, 2001, and police officers at first chuckled at the reports, thinking they were an April Fools' joke. But stories of the plummeting pup were true, yet another twist in what was already one of the country's strangest historical preservation efforts.

Doggie Diners had their day, too, but that was a generation ago, when there were about two dozen of the hot dog stands throughout San Francisco and Oakland. All of them featured the grinning, candy-apple red dachshund spinning on a pole out front. The dog sported a blue polka-dotted bow tie and white chef's hat.

But the chain fell on hard times and closed in 1986. The doggie heads were eventually sold to private owners and taken down—all except one, outside a restaurant on Sloat Boulevard at 46th Avenue, a former Doggie Diner. Preservationists had puppy eyes for the last doggie still standing and had stirred up a fierce political battle by barking at city officials to declare it a protected

This dog looks out on a bright future.

landmark. That effort failed, but the city agreed to take up ownership of the orphaned dog. City officials were making plans to shore up its perch when it fell over a year later in a storm.

The city, along with private donors, raised $25,000 to restore the dog to prime condition, including fixing up its smashed snout. During a gala ceremony it was put back in place in June, 2001. The wide-eyed pup now flashes a silly grin at passersby and gazes out at the horizon, not a landmark yet but a dog with quite a tale.

SQUATTING ON THE DOCK OF THE BAY

Pier 39 officials were at first slow to react to the golden egg tossed in their laps in the winter of 1989 when dozens of sea lions took over a dock and refused to leave. Their misgivings probably had something to do with the fact that these unwelcome guests stank, spewed nasty fish breath, barked loudly day and night, and otherwise behaved in uncivilized ways, as wild animals tend to do.

Then Pier 39 merchants noticed that the smelly intruders were attracting attention and, more importantly, tourist dollars. So they had a change of heart. After all, what's a measly old dock if it means a serious uptick in business? What's evolved since is a win-win situation: The sea lions have a snazzy place with a good food supply where they can haul out for the winter, and the pier's restaurants and shops get a major tourist attraction that doesn't require a union contract.

About 900 sea lions now winter on the pier's D dock doing what sea lions do, which isn't much. Activities include napping, cuddling, yelping, and shoving each other around during playful displays of dominance. This limited repertoire has scored big with the public. Visitors have flocked here ever since word of the sea lion invasion got out. Pier 39 officials could not have planned it any better since the sea lion population peaks during the normal low of the tourist season. It's no wonder that the pier has erected a statue in honor of the sea lions and also renamed an access path Sea Lion Way.

Two of Pier 39's sea lions share a tender moment.

Now there are bleacher seats set up for people to watch the
action. While most of the sea lions seem oblivious to the throngs,
a few hams play up to the crowd, waddling around noisily on a
platform only a few feet away from everyone. Some have settled
in so nicely that they no longer migrate south during summer.
Although most leave after winter, a few dozen now stay on per-
manently, providing the pier with a year-round tourist magnet.
For all that, putting up with their stinky breath is a small price
to pay.

THE SHORT AND WINDING ROAD

You have to question the enduring appeal of a block of Lombard Street that's known as the Crookedest Street in the World. Never mind that *crookedest* really isn't a word. Even without the catchy title, this would be one of the most famous passageways on Earth.

The stretch of Lombard between Hyde and Leavenworth Streets is a twisted journey with more curves than a Hollywood sexpot. This maddening boulevard is the least practical of roads to travel along, yet drivers just can't stay away. It consists of eight turns so radically sharp that *hairpin* hardly describes them. Cars become like slalom skiers in slow motion, shushing back and forth at a walking pace.

Despite its flaws, this is a road most traveled by, a rite of passage for tourists and coming-of-age locals with new driver's licenses. The traffic jams caused by cars waiting to make the coiling descent during peak tourist season have enraged nearby residents, and there are frequent calls to shut it down. City officials have responded by saying that if people want to drive themselves crazy by cruising Lombard, it's their legal right. The street has withstood every challenge to close it to traffic.

When the loony lane first opened in 1922 it wasn't intended to have the thrilling appeal of a roller coaster attraction. The switchbacks were created to ease the ride down the steep hill. But that's all forgotten today.

In addition to driving Lombard, a popular tradition is to stand at the bottom and pose for a souvenir photograph with the picturesque and curvaceous street in the background. If you're driving down the hill, you'll see the crowd looking up at you. You can also glimpse spectacular views of the city and bay. But this is one time you'd better keep your eyes on the road—if you can keep up with its tortuous path.

Here's one way to test your car's turning radius.

NOTE: San Francisco does have another, less famous crooked street if you want to avoid the Lombard crowds. It's Vermont Street between 20th and 22nd Streets.

THIS FORECAST IS NEVER WRONG

The Tonga Room and Hurricane Bar has the most predictable weather pattern of any place on the planet. Most of the time it's dry and comfortable, with moderate temperatures and no wind, what you'd expect from a large room that's indoors—except that every thirty minutes a violent and clamorous thunderstorm erupts and produces torrents of rain. The dramatic shift in weather happens here like clockwork because timers and machines control it all.

Rain is always in the forecast at this place.
Photo: Elissa Curtis.

The indoor storm is the major attraction of this Polynesian-themed watering hole that also features tables with thatched roof coverings, a central lagoon, and a floating stage. There's an untraditional happy hour buffet featuring Pacific Rim fare such as pot stickers, spare ribs, and pork buns. And, of course, you can order from an assortment of fruity rum concoctions that are served in tiki glasses with pineapple chunks and sweet cherries speared on drink stirrers topped with paper umbrellas.

What makes the Tonga Room so special is that it's housed within the refined splendor of the Fairmont Hotel. The pairing is about as incongruous as, well, an indoor rainstorm. The Fairmont Hotel is a marble-lined palace that has housed royalty and U.S. presidents since it first opened on Nob Hill in 1907. You pass through the gold-leaf trappings of the hotel to get to the Tonga's tropical island of kitsch. Just as you adjust to the jarring shift in atmosphere, it starts to rain—indoors. Then you know it's time to order another mai tai.

Paradise at the Tonga Room can be found at 950 Mason Street. You can call (415) 772–5278 and you just might hear the sound of a heavy rain falling in the background.

WHERE THE BUFFALO DON'T ROAM

Golden Gate Park is a refreshing urban oasis of lush meadows, small lakes, ball fields, and museums. That much you expect. What comes as a surprise to many visitors is the discovery of a herd of bison in a small paddock area at the western end of the park's John F. Kennedy Drive.

The massive beasts with the bulbous heads always seem to be having bad fur days. In fact, an earlier herd was exiled to nearby San Bruno in the 1980s because it had become too sickly and "scruffy" in appearance, according to news reports. A new herd was bought from a meat company that normally supplied a local restaurant known for its buffalo burgers.

*Golden Gate Park's buffalo have adopted
a laid-back attitude.*

Spared becoming an entree, you'd think the new herd would
kick up their hooves and savor life a bit. But these wooly animals
don't live up to their lore as wanderers. They mostly shuffle about
munching pine needles or pose majestically while kneeling on the
ground in a slumbering stance. Still, even while stationary, they
are quite a sight.

The park's bison represent a dogged preservation effort begun
in the late nineteenth century after the American buffalo, which
once numbered in the millions, had almost been wiped out by
hunters. A male and female were brought to the park in 1891 and
quickly got busy, and the herd's numbers grew steadily. The first
two buffalo were named Benjamin Harrison and Sarah Bernhardt,
beginning a tradition of naming members after well-known public figures. Later animals were named after former mayors of San

Francisco, and others took the monikers of historical figures from Shakespeare.

The San Francisco Zoo, charged with caring for the animals, says that more than 500 calves have been born at the park in the hundred-plus years they've been there.

A HEAD OF STATE, ALL IN HIS HEAD

With his feathered cap, military jacket with epaulets, and a long saber at his side, Joshua Norton certainly projected the image of an important world figure. In fact, he was America's first emperor. At least that's what he called himself, or rather, decreed. Norton was a San Francisco businessman who had lost his fortune in the rice market. One day in 1859 he walked into a newspaper office and brightened up a slow news day by handing the editor a proclamation declaring himself to be Norton I, Emperor of the United States and Protector of Mexico.

The proclamation was duly published, and so began Emperor Norton's reign, certainly one of the more colorful personal histories in a city full of eccentric characters. For the next twenty years, Norton issued decrees and paraded around San Francisco with his mongrel mutts, Bummer and Lazarus. He saluted people and was saluted back. He issued his own currency that was honored, with a wink, by local merchants. He dined for free at all city restaurants and wrote letters to officials in Washington offering to mediate in the Civil War. At every theater opening in town, three seats were left open for Norton and his dogs.

He could be grand in his decrees, or sometimes base and prosaic. He issued proclamations to dissolve all religion and the United States, while also declaring that a local hotel should give him a free room or else be banished.

Norton's decrees were popular reading, and the publication of them was good business for local newspapers, so much so that editors sometimes wrote their own to help sell papers.

Historians say that Norton was a beloved local figure who might not have been so crazy after all. He decreed in 1872 that a suspension bridge should be built connecting Oakland to San Francisco, several decades before the real one was constructed. When his dog Bummer died, Mark Twain wrote an epitaph. When Norton died in 1880, thousands attended his funeral. They say he died penniless, but, of course, he had plenty of currency in the name of Norton I.

Buy Them Some Peanuts and Life Jackets

For some San Francisco Giants fans, the best seats in the house aren't even in the house. They're not even seats really, but flotation devices such as kayaks, canoes, rafts, inner tubes, or speedboats. During each home game at the Giants' downtown baseball stadium, a crafty group of boaters gathers in a narrow channel outside the park's right-field section. It's a vantage point that affords nice views of the San Francisco Bay, but not even a glimpse of the action on the field. No matter to this crew. They set their sights on landing a most rare catch in these frigid waters—a home-run ball hit out of the stadium and into an area of the bay known as McCovey Cove, in honor of former Giants slugger Willie McCovey.

Home runs hit by a Giant over the park's 24-foot wall and into the bay are called splashdowns, and they are prized souvenirs to these floating fans, especially ones hit by the team's star, Barry Bonds. Since the park first opened in 2000, Bonds has launched the majority of home runs powered into McCovey Cove. Because he is finishing up a legendary career and setting many baseball records, many of his home-run balls are soggy but valuable pieces of baseball history.

As great a hitter as Bonds is, he manages only a handful of splashdowns each season, which means that boaters outside the

These boaters are into catching flies.
Photo: Elissa Curtis.

stadium have a lot of time on their hands. Most come prepared with ice chests of drinks and grills to barbecue up floating feasts as they party away while following the game on portable radios, televisions, and cell phones.

When a home run does make a splash, there's a mad dash for the ball, with some people diving into the water and others trying to maneuver their craft into retrieval position to scoop up the ball with fishing nets. Then the long wait begins anew.

Cameras outside the stadium capture all the action in McCovey Cove, and it has proven to be a popular sidelight at games. The exposure has made some Cove regulars celebrities around town. There is a downside. When a home run is hit, some right-field fans toss a baseball into the water to watch the mad scramble for it. When the ball is found, the boater has a momentary feeling of success, until it is examined to reveal what's written on it: Sucker.

A VALIANT PERFORMANCE
UNDER PRESSURE

San Francisco is the only city in the world that has honored a fire hydrant for heroic duty. Some residents gush with pride at the mention of the humble hose attachment, located at the intersection of Church and 20th Streets. It was here, in the aftermath of the great earthquake and fire of 1906, that firefighters made a dogged stand against a hell storm of flames heading for the Mission District. When every other hydrant failed, this reliable fireplug supplied a steady stream of water that aided the efforts to subdue the blaze and save the neighborhood.

That's heady stuff for a hydrant. The plug has been elevated to the status of Golden Hydrant. It's a symbol of civic pride and the city's spirit to rise from the ashes of that catastrophe. On every anniversary of the quake, remaining survivors gather at the hydrant to coat it with a fresh topping of golden paint. A plaque imbedded in the sidewalk tells the story of the champion plug, ensuring that its great deed won't be forgotten. A note to passing dogs: Don't even think about it.

This is one heroic hydrant.

RING LEADERS SET THE TONE FOR THIS CONTEST

San Francisco may be the only city instantly recognized by a noise—in this case, the familiar clanging of its fabled cable cars. Knowing how to properly sound the bell is as important to cable car operators as knowing how to make the cars stop and go, probably more so in this tourist town where the people who drive cable cars are just as much performers as transportation workers.

The bells are there for a purpose and not merely for the entertainment value of providing a jaunty soundtrack for a tourist visit. They are primarily used to communicate signals between the car's gripman and conductor. One bell toll from the conductor tells the gripman to stop the car. They're also sounded as warnings to pedestrians to get the heck out of the way because a cable car is coming.

But enough of that. What matters most to professional cable car bell ringers is style points. That's why each year they square off in a fiercely contested battle to determine the city's best cable car bell ringer. Contestants get a minute to sway judges with their originality, style, and overall technique. These unique concerts sound a bit like pieces of silverware rhythmically dropping to the floor.

The contest dates back to 1949 when the city held a competition to select three gripmen to operate a cable car at a Chicago railroad fair. Annual contests were started in 1955 and then discontinued during the 1960s and early 1970s but started up again in 1977. They're held each July in Union Square.

A BIG STRETCH FOR RECOGNITION

If you spend five years and hundreds of dollars toiling away to create a ball of rubber bands that weighs as much as a car, well, you ought to have a world record. That hasn't happened for Samir Keishk and Nabil Kishek, but they still have one heck of a rubber band globe. It weighs 2,800 pounds, is more than 5 feet tall, and consists of more than one million rubber bands woven together.

Would you believe this isn't the world's largest rubber band ball?

The brothers, who have different last names because of an immigration screwup, have a love-hate relationship with their colossal rubberized sphere. A sign on the outside of their Mission District corner market merrily invites people in to see "the world's biggest rubber band ball." But inside the Pride Superette their prized ball is kept under a dusty old blanket. You have to plead with them to uncover their masterpiece. "Too many people mess with it. They snap the bands," Nabil says with disgust.

The brothers are reasonably frustrated. Originally, Samir started the ball intending it as a gift for his grandson. Then he began focusing on a world record and enlisted Nabil's aid. They bought new rubber bands in bulk, carefully washing and drying them and looping them into long chains so that they would fit around the growing orb. But the giant rubber band ball category is a hotly contested world record. The brothers were beat out in 2002 by a Welsh man who had a ball that weighed 2,523 pounds. He then dropped it from a plane over Arizona as a stunt to see if it would bounce. It dented the earth and broke into pieces, giving Nabil and Samir some hope. They soon passed that record but were beat again in 2003 by an American with a new record of 3,120 pounds. It's clear the brothers will just have to keep stretching their limit to earn a world record. Stop by the store at 3398 22nd Street to see how they're coming along.

OUT OF THIS WORLD, AND INTO A CONE

There's no place to sit, the lines are usually long, and there are plenty of other places more conveniently located to get frozen treats in this ice-cream-loving city. So why is Mitchell's Ice Cream so popular? It must be the macapuno. That's sweet coconut, in case you've never been there.

Macapuno is just one of the many exotic fruit and vegetable flavors offered daily at Mitchell's on a menu that challenges conventional wisdom about ice cream. Can purple yam be an ice

Nobody outscoops this man when it comes to
oddly flavored ice cream.

cream flavor? Yes it can. It's bright purple, mildly sweet, creamy, and satisfying. Other unusual flavors here include jackfruit, lychee, and buko, or baby coconut. There are seasonal ice creams, too, such as fresh cantaloupe in the summer, pumpkin pie in the fall, and eggnog in winter. "Cantaloupe is very popular. People start asking for it in February," says Larry Mitchell, who started the shop in 1953 with his brother, Jack. Funny thing was, Larry admits he didn't know much about making ice cream back then, even though his family had run a dairy in the same neighborhood back in the 1800s. So a dairy salesman spent a week showing him the ropes. It still took some years before the shop's popularity really took off in the 1960s, if somewhat by a fluke.

The Mitchells had a friend who was importing mangoes, and they bought a bunch and turned them into ice cream. The frozen mango flavor was a hit with the neighborhood's growing population of Filipinos. Soon the Mitchells were experimenting with all kinds of otherworldly fruit and vegetable flavors in the kitchen of their shop, where all their ice cream is made daily, and they've never looked back at chocolate or vanilla since.

The shop is still a family operation, although Jack has long since retired. Larry still maintains his usual hands-on management style, one reason why there are no franchises. It would be too hard for him to keep an eye on every store. You'll just have to drop by 688 San Jose Avenue (415–648–2300) to taste for yourself.

Other exotic offerings in town include Bombay Ice Creamery at 552 Valencia Street (415–431–1103), which offers flavors such as fig, saffron rose, ginger, and cardamom, and Polly Ann's at 3142 Noriega Street (415–664–2472), which is known for vegetable-flavored ice creams such as spinach and tomato. You won't know whether to eat it from a cone or melt it over a pizza.

A RIDE ON THIS BUS IS A REAL TRIP

Are you Green Tortoise material? Let's put it another way: When you vacation, do you travel by airplane, eat at restaurants, and enjoy the comforts of a hotel? Then probably not. You are very much, in fact, anti-Tortoise.

The Green Tortoise, a unique San Francisco–based bus company, offers low-cost tours throughout America and Mexico. The catch—and it's a big one—is that you'll have to sleep on foam pads on the bus while it's rolling along at night and do your own cooking and dish washing, too. You'll also have to redefine your ideas about personal space and hygiene. Showering is of the "no-soap" variety in passing lakes and streams. There are no bathrooms aboard the buses, and sometimes the only toilet you'll be offered is a hole in the ground behind a bush along the road.

The company has transformed old Greyhound coaches into rolling communes that take up to forty people at a time on what they call "adventures travel." About half of the Tortoise folks are between the ages of eighteen and twenty-five, and only a third are Americans. On this bus it's all about the journey and meeting new people. Most riders, in fact, are single and open to mingling.

In addition, there are many stops for outdoor recreational activities such as hiking, mountain climbing, rafting, and swimming. Sometimes everyone camps outside at night. At other times drivers perform "the miracle," transforming the coach from a place to lounge during the day to sleeping quarters at night that can accommodate everyone, just barely. Getting to know fellow travelers, after all, is a big part of this adventure.

The company started in 1974 when founder Gardner Kent wanted to drive his family across the country in a school bus and sold tickets to other riders who wanted to come along. Plenty did, and that led to the creation of the Green Tortoise. This transportation service from the 1970s just keeps truckin' along. To hitch a ride, call the company at (800) 867–8647 or visit its Web site at www.greentortoise.com.

VERY SOON YOU WILL READ
ABOUT FORTUNE COOKIES

If your fate came wrapped in a cookie, would you take it to heart? Apparently yes, judging by the enduring popularity of the fortune cookie. The first fortune cookie was most likely introduced in San Francisco around 1920, making it an American invention, although it may have been inspired by the fourteenth-century tradition of Chinese soldiers passing secret messages hidden inside cakes.

The idea of offering destiny in a dessert has been a sweet success, with greater demand forcing most cookie companies to automate their operations to step up production in the twenty-first century. There are still a few shops that make the cookies by hand, and one of those is an out-of-the-way stop in Chinatown known as the Golden Gate Fortune Cookie Company. Along a clut-

This is where they seal your fate.

tered alleyway, you can peer into the cramped factory space and watch two women seated before contraptions with moving conveyer belts containing horseshoe-shaped baking tins. The tins are pulled through ovens that bake the cookie dough, and then the women pull the round pancakes from the hot press. Then, in a deft move, they slip the slivers of paper with the fated message into the flattened dough and give it a pinch to mold it into the fortune cookie's familiar bundled shape. Operators here say they can produce up to 1,000 cookies an hour this way, but the pace seems a little slower at times. Watching the process may demystify the cookie's allure. You'll come away knowing that it was a human hand that sealed your fate, and not some supernatural process. Of course, you can also come away with a bag of either chocolate or vanilla cookies.

The company provides the rare opportunity for you to act like a god by customizing your own fortune. Or you can leave your fate in someone else's hands. See your destiny being folded at 56 Ross Alley.

FILLING UP A BIG SLOT IN HIS LIFE

When Edward Zelinsky was eleven he won five quarts of oil during a drawing at a local theater, a prize that didn't interest him much. So he sold the oil and used the proceeds to buy his first penny-arcade game, fueling a lifelong passion for collecting coin-operated wonders. By the time he was an adult, Zelinsky had amassed the world's largest private collection of mechanical art. He owns more than 300 items that include antique slot machines, automated musical instruments and players, and coin-operated amusements such as mechanical fortune-tellers, peep shows, dioramas, and games.

Zelinsky shared his collection with the public by opening one of San Francisco's more unusual attractions, the Musee Mecanique. Although it is labeled a museum, there is none of that stuffy, hands-off attitude here. Visitors can admire these ancient marvels, and if they have loose change, they can play them as well. Everything displayed is in working order and comes to life when coins are inserted.

There are dioramas such as Royal Court, where tiny, elaborately-designed figures dance in a miniature, ornate French-style ballroom. More sinister are animated scenes such as the French Guillotine, where doors of a castle swing open to reveal a depiction of a beheading, and the Opium Den, where staggering, skeleton-like figures portray the harrowing effects of narcotic consumption.

On the risqué side there are several peep shows such as Susie the can-can dancer and another automated viewer that offers people a chance to "see what the belly dancer does on her day off." These salacious come-ons promise more than they deliver.

For a quarter, he'll lock arms with anybody.

The Musee features several automated musical presentations, including a box with musical monkeys, and a massive carnival show with a hundred different moving parts including a Ferris wheel, a children's plane ride, and acrobats in motion.

For more traditional arcade fare, you can appeal to mechanical fortune-tellers who spit out your fate on small cards, or test your pucker power on the Kiss-o-meter, which offers ratings from ice-cold to hot stuff. Automated antique skill games include arm-wrestling, hockey, and baseball.

It's all fun and games, with a big dose of cultural history, too. The collection is up and working at Pier 45 at the end of Taylor Street at Fisherman's Wharf. For more information you can visit the museum's Web site at www.museemechanique.org or call (415) 346–2000.

SOMETHING FUNNY ABOUT THIS HEAD COUNT

Laughing Sal is a freckle-faced, chubby chuckler with an ample bosom and a gap-tooth smile who bursts into a prolonged, boisterous, phlegm-coated cackle at the insertion of a coin. Drop her a quarter and her arms swing into jerky motion as if she's convulsing with sinister spasms of shrieking laughter. She's equal parts haunting and mirthful, and for years she entertained and horrified visitors to San Francisco's Playland at the Beach, a seaside amusement park where she was stationed at the entrance to the funhouse.

Playland closed in 1972 to make way for beachfront condos, and it seemed that Laughing Sal's chortling would become a nostalgic lament for those who fondly remembered Playland. Three decades after Playland's demise, officials at Santa Cruz's Beach Boardwalk paid $50,000 to a private collector for Playland's original Laughing Sal and set her up at their beachside park to resume her tittering ways. Then came a howl of protest from Edward Zelinsky, owner of San Francisco's Musee Mecanique, a palace of antique coin-operated amusements. He countered that he possessed Playland's original Sal, and it was part of the Musee's display. Then another San Franciscan, David Cherry, went public with a story about how he had witnessed Sal's head being ripped off its body at Playland's closing, and that he had acquired that decapitated skull for his collection. Richard Tuck stepped into the controversy by announcing that he was opening a tribute to Playland in El Cerrito to be called Playland Not At the Beach, which would include a reproduction of the park's original Laughing Sal.

The conflict raised the question of who had the real Laughing Sal, and whether four laughing heads were better than one. Meanwhile the various Sals seem unfazed by all the hullabaloo as everyone waits to see who will have the last laugh in this mystery.

When she laughs, sometimes the whole world doesn't laugh with her.

ALL THAT JAZZ ABOUT RELIGION

When Bishop Franzo King saw the great saxophonist John Coltrane perform in San Francisco's North Beach in 1965, he didn't just come away knowing he'd heard some superior tunes. Instead, he had a spiritual transformation, or a "baptism of sound," he later told the *San Francisco Weekly*.

A sign that things are different at this church.

In fact, King's newfound enlightenment was similar to the experience of Coltrane himself, who had kicked a heroin habit and then told of his own religious awakening in 1957 in the liner notes to his *Love Supreme* album. "At that time, in gratitude, I humbly asked to be given the means and privilege to make others happy through music," Coltrane wrote.

Much the same can be said of King, who two years after Coltrane's death in 1967 founded a most unusual religious group called the St. John Will-I-Am Coltrane African Orthodox Church. It's known here simply as the Church of Coltrane, and it's the only church in the world that features Coltrane's music as the main theme of its liturgy.

One thing you can say about this church's services—they are never dull. They sometimes begin with jam sessions lead by King on the tenor saxophone. These are free-flowing musical interludes that sometimes last more than an hour. Those in the congregation also bring instruments to play or simply sing along. There are also biblical readings and sermons.

Since its founding the church has taken an active role in providing food, clothing, and shelter to the needy. Then it became needy itself. Rising rents forced the church out of its longtime home in 2000. They've since found a temporary space at 930 Gough Street where they hold regular Sunday services at 11:45 A.M. Call (415) 673–3572 for more information.

THE BENEFITS OF GOING NOWHERE

The idea of going in circles suggests a frazzled state of frustration and inertia. Nothing could be more disheartening than to think you're going somewhere only to end up right back where you started. This nightmarish scenario has been given a positive spin by a growing movement of circle walkers led by the Reverend Lauren Artress of San Francisco's Grace Cathedral.

Just walking around on a nice day.

In the early 1990s Artress spearheaded efforts to revive the centuries-old tradition of walking labyrinths as a way of calming your mind. A common feature of medieval cathedrals, labyrinths were circular paths leading to a center and then back to the start that people traversed as a kind of spiritual journey, or at least to clear their heads and lift their mood. Artress visited a famous one at the thirteenth-century Chartres Cathedral in France that had been covered over by chairs and long forgotten. It became her mission to restore that one as well as initiating efforts to build them around the world.

In 1995 Grace Cathedral built the first permanent labyrinth constructed in the Western Hemisphere in 600 years, located outside the cathedral doors and made of terrazzo stone. A labyrinth of tapestry had been built a year earlier inside the cathedral.

Artress then began holding labyrinth workshops around the country to encourage others to be built. She spent a great deal of time countering the negative connotation of the word *labyrinth*, which most people rightly associated with a perplexing pattern of pathways meant to confuse and make people lose their way, akin to a maze. How could that be enjoyable and spiritually fulfilling?

But Artress countered that these labyrinths were different and intended as easy-to-follow routes in and out of a circle. By walking them you would feel energized, clear-headed, and more at peace.

Artress is hardly going in circles with her promotion efforts. They've led to hundreds of labyrinths being built around the country in diverse locations such as churches, prisons, hospitals, parks, and retirement homes. She has also founded an organization called Veriditas, known as the voice of the labyrinth movement, and written an explanatory book. The group offers unique products such as portable labyrinths that allow users to let their fingers do the walking.

For more information stroll over to her group's Web site at www.veriditas.net or call (415) 561–2921.

ART WITH A BIG HEART

You can call it a case of bovine envy. After Chicago launched the popular Cows on Parade, artistically decorated fiberglass cows displayed around town, in 1999, other cities lined up like a herd to follow in Chicago's hoofprints. Suddenly there were artworks depicting animals and even utensils turning up as public art in cities around North America, from fiberglass moose in Toronto to 6-foot-tall forks in Grand Forks, North Dakota. Take that, Chicago.

San Francisco followed suit in 2004 by announcing, appropriately on Valentine's Day, the start of Hearts in San Francisco, a plan to display dozens of 5-foot, fiberglass hearts throughout the

In San Francisco, hearts are left all over town.

city, each uniquely decorated by a different local artist. The body's blood pump was deemed a suitable icon because of the city's celebrated anthem, "I Left My Heart in San Francisco." The project may also explain what happens to hearts that get left behind—they get turned into fanciful pieces of public art.

By summer of 2004 the artfully decorated hearts were everywhere, and they were colorful, whimsical and sometimes a bit weird. *Global Heart* by Kara Maria features globs of green and blue flattened over the heart shape, while *Wolf Heart* depicts a plaid-eared wolf with bloodshot eyes wearing a bright red bib. One heart shape at Union Square has a practical side—it powers a wireless Internet connection provided by Intel.

The project is a fund-raising effort for San Francisco General Hospital. All of the hearts are sponsored by donors, and eventually will be auctioned off to the public. For more information, visit the project's Web site at www.heartsinsf.com or call (415) 651–1811.

MASTERS OF EXTERIOR DECORATING

S an Francisco probably leads the nation in the number of murals. Blank walls here cry out "Paint me!" to anyone with a brush and an artistic vision. There are more than 600 murals adorning walls, garage doors, fences, and any other available outdoor public space that can be turned into a painted canvas. Cruise a few city blocks and you're apt to feel as if you're in an art gallery instead of outdoors along a city street.

The highest concentration of this unique art form is the city's Mission District, clearly the heart of San Francisco's mural movement. The first murals began appearing here in the 1970s along

There's plenty of alfresco art in the Mission District.

Balmy Alley between Harrison and Twenty-fifth Streets, painted on garage doors and apartment walls. Murals have since spread to every conceivable space in the neighborhood, including along the walls of taquerias, churches, and corner stores.

The murals here are boldly drawn in vibrant colors and are mostly massive works expressing powerful themes. For example, on the corner of York and Twenty-fourth Streets, there is a blue-toned tableau depicting provocative images of police oppression. Other works celebrate the neighborhood's Latino culture or are more spiritual and religious in nature.

The Precita Eyes Mural Arts Center at 2981 Twenty-fourth Street has helped foster the mural movement here, offering classes and tours. You can go on a guided walk with someone from the center and see seventy-five murals in only a six-block tour.

The group also sponsors the annual mural awareness month of May, an event that features painting contests and a live mural performance where an artist will create a mural in an afternoon. For more information contact the group at (415) 285–2287 or visit them online at www.precitaeyes.org.

A Serious Look at the Funny Papers

Saturday-morning cartoons and the Sunday comics are good for a few laughs. Do they also qualify as art? That's what some cartoon fans believe. They've created a Louvre of Looney Tunes known as the Cartoon Art Museum. It's the only museum in the country dedicated to cartoon art in all its forms.

The museum began in 1984 as a traveling show, but now, thanks to an endowment from *Peanuts* creator Charles Schulz that was more than just peanuts, they've got a permanent space. The museum has more than 6,000 original pieces of cartoon art, a research library, a bookstore, and a classroom for lectures.

It's okay to laugh as you study some of the comic-strip panels hung like fine art, framed and illuminated with track lighting on

From the funny papers to a museum wall.

an expanse of white wall. But, perhaps swept up by the studious museum setting, you may also find yourself considering the artistic and cultural merits of, say, a *Calvin and Hobbes* panel or even one from *The Family Circus*. Framed cels from animation feature classics such as *Snow White* and *Pinocchio* are easily admired in this environment and appreciated for their artistic appeal.

The museum tackles the weighty world of political cartoons, too. One special exhibit highlighted the powerful satiric work featured in *The Wasp*, a political cartoon weekly published from 1876 to 1897. The cartoons displayed presented scathing attacks on political and cultural figures of the day, such as Leland Stanford and Oscar Wilde.

The museum likes to profile cartoonists and present the scope of their work, such as an exhibit on Johnny Gruelle. While best known for creating Raggedy Ann and Andy, he was an illustrator who did much more. The museum exhibited some of his other works, as well as vintage dolls, toys, and animation art based on his characters.

A visit to the museum at 655 Mission Street should foster a greater appreciation for cartoon art. Call 415–CARTOON (227–8666) for more information.

THESE ARTWORKS ARE JUST PLAIN GARBAGE

San Franciscans tossing away old shoes, used wrappers, or worn tires may just think they're taking out the trash. In reality they also may be collaborating on an art project. That's because of one of the country's most unique artist-in-residence programs. Since 1990 the SF Recycling and Disposal Company, which runs the city dump, has hired several San Francisco Bay Area artists to fill the unique position of artist-in-residence at its recycling plant and trash collection site.

While it may not seem like a prized opportunity to some, these artists get unlimited access to all of the city's garbage to use as raw material for their creative imaginations. The position does have a decided upside, such as the use of a studio on the company's forty-four-acre facility and access to of all kinds of fancy equipment, such as cranes, welding apparatus, power tools, and a glass kiln. There's also an honorarium.

Artists selected to the program spend three months on-site sorting through trash and creating their works, often fanciful sculptures. One artist even used items such as discarded zippers and tape to make a formal evening gown and trashed Venetian blinds to construct a tiara. There is a reception for the artists at the end of their stint.

Conehead Seating *by Norma Yorba, an example of*
art from the city's dump.
Photo: Paul Fresina

Works created through the program are displayed in what has
to be one of the most unusual sculpture gardens in the country, a
hillside setting at the dump. There are also scheduled tours of the
garden where you get the chance to talk with the artist-in-
residence. For more information call (415) 330–1414 or view some
of the works online at the company's Web site at www.sunset
scavenger.com.

GETTING PUMPED UP ABOUT HISTORIC PUMPS

*W*hen San Franciscans decided in the late nineteenth century that they needed an urban recreational area to rival New York's Central Park, they couldn't have picked a more challenging terrain to build it on. The verdant landscape of gardens, trees, meadows, and fields now know as Golden Gate Park was mostly a wasteland of shifting sand when the park was first planned.

The city built two towering windmills along the coast to provide the massive amounts of water needed to support vegetation to tame this inhospitable environment. They constructed the Dutch windmill in 1902 to the north and the Murphy windmill in 1905 to the south. Together these mills pumped more than 70,000 gallons of water an hour from underground wells for the next two decades as the park took shape. Then the mills were shut down and left as photo props for snapshot-taking tourists who began flocking to the popular park.

While the Dutch windmill received some cosmetic work in the 1980s, the mills were in a state of severe disrepair by the start of the twenty-first century. Then a major renovation effort was finally begun. The endeavor is so sincere that parts from the windmills were shipped to a company in the Netherlands, a family-owned operation that has been in the windmill business since 1868 for restoration. The plan is for both mills, with sails over 100 feet long, to be working by 2005 so they can be demonstrated to the public. Visitors will also be able to step inside and watch the massive machinery churning. At last, it seems, the city is finally paying needed attention to the hard-working machines that helped shape one of its greatest treasures.

This old windmill helped turn Golden Gate Park green.

A BURNING CONTROVERSY ENGULFS A FAMILIAR LANDMARK

Coit Tower is a clearly visible and easily recognized city sight from its perch atop Telegraph Hill. Not so clear is the intent of the architect who designed it.

When it was dedicated in 1933, the 210-foot tower struck many San Franciscans as looking like a giant fire hose nozzle. That would be fitting enough, since the late Lillie Hitchcock Coit donated the funds to build it. Coit was a wealthy financier's wife and a lifelong supporter of the San Francisco Fire Department, especially her beloved Knickerbocker Engine Company No. 5.

If this monument isn't a fire nozzle, what is it?

As a kid she had stopped on her way home from school to help the engine company put out a blaze. She maintained a lifelong fascination with the dashing firefighters and their snazzy uniforms. She often hung out as one of the guys, playing cards and smoking cigars, and visited them in hospitals if they were injured. She was voted an honorary member of the Knickerbocker crew in 1863. Some have even suggested that the tower's cylindrical shape and tapered end was more of a tribute to her affection for the manhood of these gallant firemen.

Amid the snickers, architect Arthur Brown Jr. tried for years to douse rumors that his prized work was actually a re-creation of a fire-hose nozzle. But the perception has been impossible to extinguish.

You can judge for yourself with a visit to the tower, which also contains magnificent Works Progress Administration murals within. You can visit at 1 Telegraph Hill Boulevard, or call (415) 362–0808 for more information.

THE BRAWN BEHIND A CITY'S BEAUTIFUL FEATURE

This city's signature tune, "I Left My Heart in San Francisco," speaks poetically of a place where "little cable cars climb halfway to the stars." What the song never explains is how those little cars make it up all those really big hills. It's a song about love, after all, not mechanical energy.

For a less romantic but more scientific tribute to this city's trademark transportation, you have to visit the Cable Car Museum. It's here that you'll learn more than you probably need to know about what powers those quaint cars up the city's steep inclines and around all those sharp turns. You'll get a good slice of history through exhibits of photographs and artifacts such as a vintage fare box, ticket puncher, and old tokens. You can even

The pulleys do the work, the cable cars get all the glory.

examine the world's oldest cable car, a Clay Street Hill Railroad Car Number 8 from 1873, the only surviving car from this line. This is also the year cable car service began in San Francisco.

More dramatically, the museum is housed in a working power-house, so you get to see the guts behind all the glory of the cable car system. You can gaze at the impressive heavy machinery—including motors, cables. and pulleys—that drives the whole operation. All four cables that power the city's cars enter and leave through this building and are in constant motion at a rate of 9.5 miles per hour. Grips in the cars use a device that looks like a large pair of pliers to attach the car to the cable if they want to go forward. To stop, without getting too technical, they simply let go and then apply a brake.

Historical exhibits also explain that horses were once used to pull the cars in the system's early days. But they couldn't make it up the hills. They also left behind a dirty mess on the streets. Not a very romantic picture.

Take a ride over to the museum at 1201 Mason Street. Just follow the cable. For more information call (415) 474–1887 or visit cablecarmuseum.org.

How to Stay Dry While Moving through Water

The best way to learn about sea creatures is to dive into the water and watch marine life unfold in its natural setting. That means scuba equipment and dive training, and let's face it: It's not for everyone. A painless and dry alternative to getting a diver's-eye view of underwater life is Pier 39's Aquarium of the Bay. Opened in 1996 and renovated in 2001, the aquarium offers a combination conveyer-belt ride and underwater adventure. Here you dive into the water by taking a short elevator ride. Then you step onto a slow-moving walkway that pulls you through two acrylic tube tunnels where you are surrounded by more than 700,000 gallons of seawater teeming with hundreds of fish from the San Francisco Bay.

You won't feel like Jacques Cousteau or anything, but you don't need a mask and you'll be breathing through your own nostrils, not some air tube. The view is quite spectacular, and with so little effort on your part. You don't even have to walk. Everything from giant schools of silvery anchovies to flounder, bat rays, and sturgeons cruise by on every side as you constantly swivel your head to take in all the underwater scenery. There are even several varieties of sharks and a giant Pacific octopus lurking about.

This place is totally tubular.

It takes about thirty minutes to pass through the tunnel, unless you pause occasionally to hop off the walkway to inspect something more closely, such as one of the many starfish stuck to the side of the acrylic tube. You return to the surface by way of another elevator ride without a care about getting the bends. There you'll find some touch pools where you can pet leopard sharks and bat rays. Then a final stop at a gift shop, certainly not a typical end to most scuba dives. For more information contact the aquarium at (415) 623–5353.

WHERE REDWOOD TREES AND CABLE CARS STAND BETWEEN YOU AND TEN PINS

Ah yes, the majestic scenery of Yosemite. It just makes you want to . . . bowl? While turning Yosemite National Park into a bowling alley would make naturalist John Muir turn over in his grave, it's a reality of sorts at the Metreon Entertainment Center. The latest in computer technology meets up with the traditional low-tech world of recreational bowling at an attraction called HyperBowl.

HyperBowl offers the opportunity for users to turn settings such as the streets of San Francisco and Tokyo, a roiling pirate ship, and even hallowed Yosemite Park into virtual bowling alleys that show up on a big screen. Bowlers here bend over a real bowling ball and then frantically spin and turn it to control a virtual ball that rolls along the screen toward computer-projected pins. In the San Francisco game, for example, bowlers have to navigate their ball down and then up major hills while avoiding urban obstacles such as buildings, fire hydrants, and moving cable cars. You also have a limited time to get the ball to the pins or you score a zero. The only thing similar to this and real bowling is that the scoring is the same.

San Francisco's HyperBowl was the first offering of its kind in the country, although it's now catching on elsewhere and is also available as a home version as well. Strike out for 101 Fourth Street to get the full original experience. Call (415) 369–6013 or click on www.metreon.com for more information.

Going where no bowling ball has gone before.

SAN FRANCISCO BAY AREA

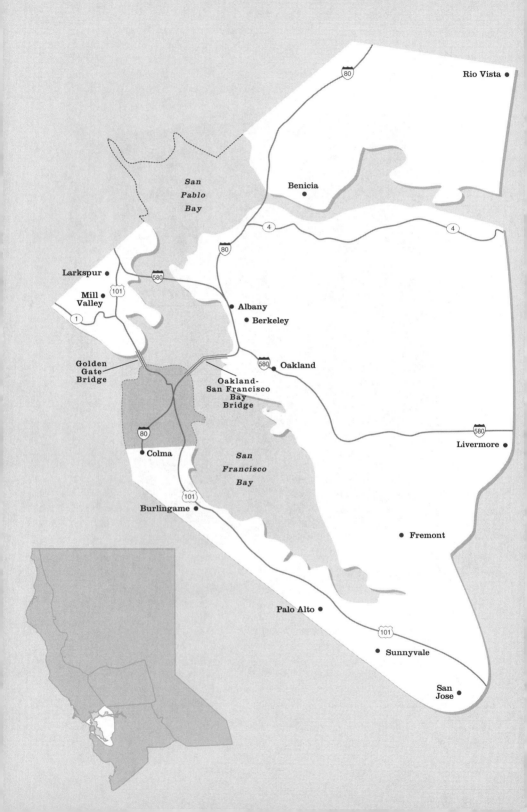

San Francisco Bay Area

THE CROONING COP
Albany

There are Elvis impersonators, and then there is Bill Palmini, a police lieutenant known around the station as "Elvis" Palmini. The nickname stems from Palmini's stage persona, a safety-conscious Elvis who quivers his lips in the name of promoting better driving habits.

Sure, anyone can swivel his hips like the King, but only Palmini belts out Elvis tunes such as "Don't Be Cruel" while inserting safe-driving messages into his delivery. That's how Palmini launched his act in 1991, the first time he shed his police blues for a white sequined jumpsuit. His unusual act has earned him a hunk of publicity and made him the only known cop in history to earn a gold record, even if it is honorary.

Palmini became the key feature of a state-funded young-driver safety program, appearing at hundreds of school assemblies to treat students to the unusual sight of an animated, glittering former singing idol crooning about the importance of wearing seat belts. He has recorded public-service announcements a la Elvis that are broadcast to drivers in several states as part of highway safety programs. He's also done an album.

In between gigs Palmini used his suspicious mind to perform solid police work as Albany's chief investigator. He retired in 2003. At last report, however, his Elvis routine hasn't left the building. He continues to make public appearances, belting out tunes such as his hit recording, "One Way Road." You can hear it on the safety program's Web site at www.ubco.org.

A SPITTING IMAGE FROM THE PAST
Benicia

This town certainly has bona fide historical roots. It briefly served as the state capital from 1853 to 1854. And word of a gold discovery at Sutter's Mill first circulated at a Benicia general store in 1848, setting off a massive rush of fortune seekers and leading to California's statehood.

Benicia is also linked with a less illustrious saga in American history involving a short-lived and miserably unsuccessful experiment with camel transportation. The U.S. military briefly employed several dozen camels imported from the Near East in

These racing camels are not a mirage.
Photo: Courtesy Benicia Historical Museum.

1856 in the hopes that the humped creatures would excel in arduous treks through the western deserts and badlands. These were heady days for camel supporters, who envisioned the charge of a camel cavalry and even a camel express for delivering mail. In the end the beasts proved too burdensome to handle, and the herd was sent to Benicia in 1864 for auction.

Historians aren't clear on exactly what happened next, but the camels probably spent a couple of months at the Benicia Arsenal, a historic place in its own right. The arsenal, opened in 1849, was one of the West's earliest military posts and served through several wars before closing in 1965.

Legend has it that the camels were stabled at two warehouses at the Benicia Arsenal before they were sold off, and these building are now called the camel barns. While the camels' stay here was short, they haven't been forgotten. A historical museum at the camel barns pays tribute to them, and the city began hosting annual camel races in early summer as a further link to its dromedary past. For more information trek over to www.benicia historicalmuseum.org.

NOT IN SHIP SHAPE
Benicia

We know what happens to old soldiers. But what about old military sea vessels? It turns out they don't fade away gracefully.

Many of them end up tethered to storage docks in Benicia, floating aimlessly until the day they might be cannibalized for spare parts and dismantled for scrap. This ghost flotilla is known as the Suisun Bay Reserve Fleet. About one hundred decommissioned military craft are docked here, including guided missile cruisers, submarines, barges, oil tankers, and Coast Guard icebreakers. The site here is one of three in the United States maintained by the maritime branch of the U.S. Department of Transportation.

These ships saw plenty of action—once.
Photo: U.S. Department of Transportation, Maritime
Administration.

While these ships are sometimes derisively referred to as the
mothball fleet, many had distinguished military careers and so
have great stories to tell. Take the *Hoga*, for example. The tug-
boat began U.S. Navy service in 1941 and was stationed at Pearl
Harbor when the Japanese attacked. The *Hoga* was used to put
out fires and rescue stranded American seamen. After serving in
World War II and the Korean War, the *Hoga* was loaned to Oakland, where she served for five decades as a fireboat. The aging
but dependable tug was placed "out of service" in 1996 and
charted a course for Benicia as its possible final resting place.

Some ships are maintained here for military use as part of the
navy's Ready Reserve Force, which means they could be rushed
into service in an emergency. Others are headed for the scrap

heap unless they can get sponsors. Sometimes former shipmates step up for their old vessels. Such was the case with the SS *Jeremiah O'Brien,* which made it out of mothballs and is now docked at Pier 45 in San Francisco as a floating museum.

Former crew of the *Glacier,* an icebreaker that went on dozens of Arctic and Antarctic missions, work as volunteers taking care of the ship and are raising money to find it a permanent home. Support is also growing for a campaign to save the *Hoga,* the last surviving ship from the Pearl Harbor attack.

Art That Really Moves People
Berkeley

S ome car owners crave accessories such as leather seats, sunroofs, and powerful engines. Artist and filmmaker Harrod Blank dreamed of doors with painted roosters and bumpers adorned with musical instruments. Blank is not alone in thinking a car is more than just a way to get around. To some it is a vehicle for expression that's now a bona fide art genre, thanks in large part to Blank's promotional efforts.

Blank is an ambassador for the art car movement. He's produced two popular documentaries and a book about art cars and their creators. To promote his first film, *Wild Wheels,* Blank drove his "Oh My God!" car to screenings around the country, the vehicle that is painted like a giant beach ball and features a TV on the roof and plastic fruit and maracas on the bumpers. Needless to say, the film tour garnered much publicity. Blank's promotional skills are also evident in his organization of ArtCar Fest in the San Francisco Bay Area, an annual gathering of auto artists that features an attention-grabbing art car caravan.

Blank has received the most attention for his Camera Van, a 1972 Dodge van with close to 2,000 cameras glued to its exterior, including some patterned on the roof to spell the word *smile.* Some of the cameras actually work, controlled from instruments

This van takes moving pictures.
Photo: Hunter Mann.

inside the vehicle. Blank has taken hundreds of pictures that capture the wondered stares of people he meets on the road.

For more information on the ArtCar Fest, cruise over to www.artcarfest.com or learn more about Blank's cars at www. cameravan.com.

THE BARE TRUTH ABOUT THE LIMITS OF FREE EXPRESSION
Berkeley

The Naked Guy came to class with his books. He even donned sandals. He just didn't wear any clothes.

The Naked Guy was a University of California at Berkeley student in 1992 named Andrew Martinez, and he really tested Berkeley's famed tolerance for diverse lifestyles. The ultimate lesson of Naked Guy's educational experience was that there is such a thing as going too far, even in Berkeley.

Following a student-conduct hearing that Martinez attended in the buff, the school expelled him for his unconventional attire. School officials claimed his nakedness was disruptive in the classroom. Hey, at least teachers would know he wasn't cheating on exams.

Then Naked Guy got under the skin of city officials when he showed up as his traditional bare self at a city council meeting. Red-faced council members promptly passed a controversial law outlawing public nudity in 1993. Sure enough, Martinez was the first person arrested when it took effect.

Open-minded jurors, not wishing to squash anyone's desire to cavort unclothed around town, have been reluctant to convict anyone, making enforcement of the law difficult for city officials.

After many failed attempts, the city finally earned a conviction in 2000 of two members of a group of professional nudists known as the X-Plicit Players. The Berkeley-based group hasn't been convinced to dress up despite the ruling. They continue to host several events around town to commemorate nudity, including the annual Nude and Breast Freedom Parade, held in Berkeley's People's Park. The event celebrates the "liberation of the body from boring fashion," according to the group's Web site, at www.xplicitplayers.com

A FEEDING FRENZY
Berkeley

"One, two, three—latch!" Following these instructions, more than 1,000 mothers gathered in the Berkeley Community Theater in August 2002 to soothe their hungry babies and, more importantly, set a new world record for mass breast-feeding.

The collective nursing not only quenched a lot of infant appetites, it also eclipsed a previous mark set by 767 women in Australia. The final Berkeley tally was 1,128 suckling babies, according to event organizer Ellen Sirbu, a city nutritionist.

Sirbu acknowledged that the event was a way of going one up, lactation-wise, on the Australian group of women. But she also wanted to spotlight the benefits of breast feeding and encourage other American cities to hold similar events.

In addition to establishing the breast-feeding mark, Berkeley also set another perhaps inadvertent milestone: Biggest mass baby burping.

A CALL FOR THE WILD
Berkeley

Berkeley is more a state of mind than a real place. Oh sure, it's a city, with a mayor, police department, and streets and stuff, but it's also a symbol for ultraliberal ideals and outright zaniness. It's a place where all politics are worldly. Fittingly, Berkeley was the scene for the birth of the free-speech movement in the 1960s.

So when locals organized a parade and festival in 1996 with the provocative title "How Berkeley Can You Be?," myriad wacky acts and personalities answered the challenge. Held each fall, the

One of the more tame acts at this zany Berkeley parade.
Photo: John Solomon.

unconventional procession has showcased marching oddities such as a precision lawn-chair brigade and a group of pregnant women promenading with synchronized contractions.

This is exactly the kind of far-reaching diversity and bizarre behaviors organizer John Solomon had in mind when he conceived of the event. Solomon partly wanted to draw attention to the sometimes-neglected section of town around University Avenue, where he owns an Italian cafe and the parade is held. But more importantly, Solomon anticipated that the affair would show everyone the true meaning of Berkeley-style diversity. "I was hoping to have university Nobel laureates riding in convertibles along with dope-smoking hippies," he said. That hasn't happened yet, but every year there's a nude marching group of performance artists and another float that features meat-eating marchers. The latter group once used a bazooka to shoot chicken legs into the crowd. They also offered cigarettes to children. Like we said, this is a town known for pushing boundaries. Way out for most people is just the norm for Berkeley.

Solomon's cafe sponsors a float that catapults giant meatballs onto a colossal plate. By comparison with other acts, that hardly seems outrageous. A festival with music, food, and more uncanny happenings follows the parade. For more information march over to www.howberkeleycanyoube.com.

LIFTING SPIRITS, HAT BY HAT
Berkeley

Stacy Samuels figures he's done his part to make the world a better place. It's selling a propeller-topped beanie hat. "It's really a fun hat," he insists. "It not only sits on your head, it does something. It's the most fun hat in the world."

Yes, a hat so fun that he's built a business and a persona around it. Samuels calls himself the Chief Flight Commander and President of Interstellar Propeller, which has sold more than a million and a half propeller caps since Samuels started the company in the late 1970s.

While not the inventor of the flying beanie, Samuels has certainly propelled its popularity. Demand for propeller hats took off in the early 1990s, and other entrepreneurs threw their hats into the ring and gave Samuels some competition. Now the prop caps are popular with computer geeks, sometimes referred to as "propeller heads." They buy the caps as a sign of pride.

Samuels began selling the caps at Oakland A's games in the late 1970s when he developed the alternate persona of Super A, donning an A's propeller cap and green and gold cape while strumming a banjo to whip the crowd into a frenzy. He's as recognizable to fans as the team's star players. During football season he treks across the bay, changes the colors of his cape, and

Is it a bird or a plane? No, it's Super Niner.
Photo: Courtesy Stacy Samuels

morphs into Super Niner. As a 49ers fan he was immortalized in
football's Hall of Fame as part of a twenty-minute video shown
regularly at the shrine. He calls this fleeting moment of stardom
"a lifetime achievement."

Samuels, a former resident of California's famed Hog Farm
commune, never envisioned life as a cap capitalist years ago, but
it has turned out just fine. "Out of all the businesses I could have
done, it's good to know that I've had a positive effect on the
world," he says.

For more information propel yourself over to www.propeller
headhats.com.

FLIPPING THEIR LIDS OVER PIECES OF CANDY
Burlingame

Gary and Nancy Doss planned on selling computers. Really they did. In fact, the sign on their store still says *Computer Spectrum*. But, as Gary points out, "We haven't sold a computer in eight years."

Their lack of sales is due to Pez mania. Soon after they opened their store, they became distracted by collecting vintage Pez dispensers. When they displayed some in the store, their customers seemed to respond more to the Pez than the PCs. That's when the store morphed into the Museum of Pez Memorabilia.

Plenty of Pez at this place.

Photo: Burlingame Museum of Pez Memorabilia

Gary and Nancy were tapping into a widespread fascination with Pez dispensers, the slim plastic canisters developed to dole out the tiny brick-shaped candies. Pez candy was created in 1927 as an aid to help people quit smoking, but it took off in the United States in the early 1950s when the candy was sold with cartoon-head dispensers. Now vintage Pez dispensers are highly collectible, making the Pez museum a popular stop with Pez enthusiasts.

"Everybody seems to have fond memories of Pez. It's a cartoon toy and a candy, all in one," Gary says.

Some vintage Pez containers now sell for hundreds of dollars. Gary says the museum carries every Pez dispenser ever made, almost 500 in all. The collection includes rarities such as the Luv Pez, which looks like a giant eyeball in a hand, and the Make-A-Face Pez, which was quickly recalled from stores because its removable tiny parts were deemed a safety hazard.

Museum visitors can browse vintage Pez dispensers displayed on old toothbrush racks or purchase Pez memorabilia in the gift shop. Open up the world of Pez online at http://spectrumnet .com/pez, or head over for a closer look at 214 California Drive. Phone (650) 347–2301 for more information.

H O M E   O F   T H E   G R A V E S
C o l m a

Residents of this tiny town just south of San Francisco get lots of free perks, such as cable TV, tickets to sporting events, and summer camp for kids. There's also a golf course, card club, and scenic views. As the city slogan says, "It's great to be alive in Colma."

Yes, it's great to be alive in Colma because here it's great to be alive, period. The majority of souls here are already dead. Colma is a necropolis, the final resting place of an estimated two million people. The living population numbers around 1,200. That makes

If you want a quiet town, Colma is for you.

Colma a truly unique community, the only one in America where the dead outnumber the living. And in Colma, it's not even close. That's why the city has many morbid nicknames, including "City of the Dead," "City of Souls," and "City of the Silent."

Colma's incorporation in 1924 resulted from a ban on burials in San Francisco due to rising land values in the early 1900s. There are seventeen cemeteries in the city's 2 square miles, and some contain famous folks, including Wyatt Earp, Levi Strauss, and William Randolph Hearst. There's even a pet cemetery that is the final resting place of Tina Turner's dog. Yes, there's plenty of lively history here, and almost all of it can be found underground.

THE CAT WITH THE CHIP COMES BACK

*I*t's not that Chris Inglis ever forgot about his lost cat, Ted. It's just that after ten years, he had moved on with his life, as in new wife, new house, two daughters and replacement pets including a dog, geckos, crayfish, and a twenty-five-pound cat named Max.

Then he got a call in 2003 from the Peninsula Humane Society animal shelter telling him that they had found his lost cat. What lost cat?, Inglis asked, thinking they meant Max. No, not that cat, they told him, the other one. Ted. Missing for ten years.

Ted was a pound cat with stringy black fur that Inglis had adopted when he was divorced and living in Burlingame. Ted liked to hang out at a nearby dental office during the day and then sleep with Inglis in his waterbed at night. And they liked to take drives together, with Ted putting his paws up on the dash.

Ted ran away once, so Inglis had an identification microchip implanted in him in case he took off again. Sure enough, Ted scampered again in 1993, but was never found. A saddened Inglis scoured the neighborhood, put up lost signs, and frequently checked his favorite hangouts, but no Ted.

No news until a telephone call ten years later from the shelter, which had traced Ted to a somewhat skeptical Inglis through the cat's implanted identification chip. Inglis picked up Ted at the shelter and knew he had the right feline when Ted did his trademark paw stance on the dash as they drove away.

The story of Ted's long road back made international headlines and created a media frenzy at the Inglis household. Maybe it was because Inglis had named Ted after one of the lead characters in Bill and Ted's Excellent Adventure, and so reporters could talk about how this long wandering cat must have had an excellent adventure on his own during his ten-year absence.

Inglis, hoping that Ted wouldn't inspire him to think of another movie title such as The Great Escape, is persuading Ted with cans of tuna to put his wandering days behind him.

A FLICKERING MOMENT AS THE HEART
OF SCREENLAND
Fremont

A town with movie stars, film crews, and frequent cries of "Action!" can only be one place in California . . . Fremont? While Hollywood has long been synonymous with the film industry, Fremont was an early contender for that distinction. That's due to one hard-working movie company that opened shop in Fremont's Niles district in the early days of film. Dozens of employees of the Essanay Film Manufacturing Company descended upon this small railroad town in 1912 and produced cowboy "one-reelers" at a phenomenal rate. For the next four years the company churned out close to 400 silent films, sometimes making five or six a week.

George Spoor and Gilbert "Broncho Billy" Anderson were the *S* and *A* partners behind the studio. Anderson was the screen's first Western movie star. Essanay scored its first coup with the signing of Charlie Chaplin, who came to Niles and perfected his waddling screen persona here by filming *The Tramp*. The movies made here were mostly shot along Main Street or nearby scenic Niles Canyon. Residents often served as extras and sometimes offered possessions as props.

When Chaplin left Essanay over a contract squabble in 1916, the company disbanded and the center of the film business moved south to Hollywood, ending Niles's brief reign as a major player. Locals haven't forgotten the studio's or Chaplin's historic connection to the town. There's an annual film festival and Charlie Chaplin Day when several of the films shot here are presented in a school auditorium with piano accompaniment. For more information visit the town's Web site at www.niles.org.

A Past That Keeps Cropping Up
Fremont

Once it was nothing special to live on a farm. Only a century ago over half of all Americans did. Feeding the chickens and slopping the hogs were common pastimes.

In the last hundred years, America has seen its agrarian past slip away faster than a greased pig. Now less than 2 percent of Americans reside on a farm, meaning we're a nation of cell phone–lugging city slickers who would be clueless if challenged to milk a cow.

To get a farm fix today, you have to head to attractions such as the Ardenwood Historic Farm. At this 205-acre spread, life goes on as if the last few decades of technology development never happened. The time-warp tour includes a blacksmith station, volunteers dressed in nineteenth-century rural fashions, farm critters, wagon rides, and other assorted agrarian experiences long forgotten.

The farm is part of a huge estate once owned by George Patterson, who came west in 1849 to seek gold and ended up becoming rich as a successful planter. Visitors don't just watch—they're expected to chip in with chores, from planting crops to feeding animals. There are many special programs offered throughout the year as well, including fall harvest festivals and a Victorian Christmas celebration. The site also houses a railroad museum. To learn more ride a horseless carriage over to 34600 Ardenwood Boulevard. or use the modern convenience of a computer and check out www.ebparks.org/parks/arden.htm.

A NO-BAKED IDEA
Larkspur

No one complains about the food being underdone at Roxanne's. Or overcooked for that matter. In fact, entrees aren't cooked at all here in the conventional sense. And yet the eatery is one of the hottest around, with reservations required weeks in advance.

Roxanne's offers only raw meals, or in the parlance of followers, living foods. Eating raw food is a burning health trend, and chef Roxanne Klein is credited with being the first restaurateur in the United States to elevate this crude cooking style to gourmet levels.

Klein is a classically trained chef and vegetarian who discovered the benefits of eating uncooked meals from actor Woody Harrelson, who advised her to try it for a month. She did, and never felt better. Leaving ovens and stove tops out of meal preparation, supporters say, keeps valuable proteins and enzymes in the food.

Most people steered to a healthier diet often lament the loss of taste in their new regime. That's where Klein is recognized as a creative genius, making indulgences such as pizza and ice cream from nontraditional raw sources, such as nut milk and coconut meat. She doesn't use meat, fish, or dairy, and nothing is heated to a temperature above 118 degrees. Instead, she and her staff process herbs and organic fruits and vegetables in an array of juicers and food processors to yield tasty uncooked treats that have drawn raves from critics and diners. Klein is truly a marvel if she can never turn on an oven and still be mentioned in *Gourmet* magazine as one of the best chefs in America.

To sample a plate yourself, make reservations for the restaurant at 320 Magnolia Avenue by calling (415) 924–5004, or learn more at the detailed Web site www.roxraw.com.

BRIDGING A
LIFE SPAN

*A*l Zampa once told a reporter that to be a
bridge worker you had to be "as surefooted as
a mountain goat, agile like a cat, and be able to climb
like a monkey." Zampa was all of that during a long
career as an ironworker who helped build some of San Francisco Bay's most famous spans, including the Bay Bridge and
the Golden Gate.

Mostly sure-footed, Zampa is best remembered for one misstep
on wet iron he took in 1936 while constructing the Golden Gate. He
fell more than 40 feet, fortunately into a net, a modern safety device
in this most dangerous and often lethal profession. The net saved his
life, but it sagged under his weight and he hit the rocky shore below
and broke four vertebrae. Years later he recounted the fall to CBS
News and said: "I hit the rocks and bounced. And the first time it did-
n't seem so hard, but when I came down a second time, whoo—that's
when it hurt."

After a lengthy recovery, Zampa got right back on the bridge, yet
another indication of the pluck that made him a hero in Crockett,
where he spent most of his life. He began bridge work when he was
twenty, working on a cantilever span over the Carquinez Straight.
He worked on a second Carquinez bridge completed in 1958. At
ninety-four, long retired, he attended a ground-breaking ceremony
in 2000 for a replacement bridge over the Carquinez. He died
soon after the event. That bridge was completed in 2003 and
fittingly named in his honor. The Al Zampa Memorial Bridge
is a mile long but represents a lifetime for one rare bridge
worker who slipped and fell from the Golden Gate and
lived to tell about it.

DIGITAL DEBRIS
Livermore

S ellam Ismail's first computer was, he admits, a "dinky" little machine with very little memory. As a teenager, he sold it in the early 1980s to raise enough money to buy his second computer, an Apple II. Parting with his first machine is something he deeply regrets, and he's kept every other one since. He's also bought hundreds of other computer relics on his way to amassing what's probably the world's largest collection of vintage computers. He has 2,000 of them, ranging from a 1965 PDP 8 to more modern iMacs of the 1990s.

Each year Americans junk millions of old computers, discarding them for the next slicker and faster machine. It's been left to collectors such as Ismail to salvage this history from the scrap heap. He's an expert on early computing and has parlayed that knowledge to start a computer consulting firm called VintageTech. The company loans vintage equipment to film and photography projects and helps people retrieve data stored in obsolete formats.

Ismail is also the founder of the Vintage Computer Festival, an annual event that proves he is not alone in his fascination with items like the Apple I, the machine that launched the personal-computer age in 1976. Lots of people drop by to reminisce about the early days of wimpy PCs and monotone computer games. They gawk over dozens of old computers and swoon over ancient memory boards and worn floppy disk drives. Past programs have included a flea market of vintage computer stuff and even a "nerd trivia contest."

The festival is usually held in Silicon Valley and recently was presented at the Computer History Museum in Mountain View, a prime destination for viewing computer artifacts and learning about the early days of computing. The museum is located at

Sellam Ismail prefers the oldest and slowest computers.
Photo: Courtesy Sellam Ismail.

1401 North Shoreline Boulevard and can be reached by calling
(650) 810–1010. For more information about the festival, use your
modern high-speed connection to surf over to www.vintage.org.

A CURSE ONLY A PLUMBER COULD LOVE
Livermore

A dam Fortunate Eagle Nordwall uttered a dire warning when he stormed out of a city council meeting here in the early 1970s, threatening to put a curse on the city's sewer system. Council members probably viewed the comment as another publicity stunt by the local businessman and American Indian activist— except that two weeks later the city's sewage system really did clog up, just as Nordwall had warned. The incident is known around here as the Livermore curse, and it's had remarkable staying power.

Nordwall is best known around the Bay Area as a leader of a group of American Indian protesters who took over Alcatraz Island in 1969 and demanded that the federal government give it to all American Indians. The takeover dragged on for months and eventually lost steam, and federal agents finally reclaimed the island. Nordwall's book, *Heart of the Rock,* recounts the episode.

Around Livermore, however, Nordwall is more closely associated with the curse. Nordwall's irritation with Livermore officials stemmed from what the city did after he donated a totem pole to commemorate Livermore's centennial. The pole showed the city's founder, Robert Livermore, sitting under an eagle and featured several carved depictions of moments in Livermore's hundred-year history. It was 18 feet tall—until city workers chopped it down and encased it in cement in order to prepare it for display. Thinking the city had literally done a hatchet job to his art, Nordwall demanded that the pole be restored to its original height. When the city council said no, the famous sewer system curse was uttered.

While the city's sewage system eventually cleared, the curse remains potent.

Nordwall's totem pole is displayed in the city's tiny triangular Centennial Park. In 1999 city officials went there to dig up a his-

Is this totem pole behind Livermore's dreaded curse?

toric time capsule buried near the totem pole but, much to their embarrassment, they couldn't find it. Cursed again.

The curse was also revisited in a recent documentary on Livermore in which Nordwall and several city officials are interviewed about the historic incident. Nordwall insists in the film that the curse hasn't been lifted. Sure enough, within a few weeks of the documentary's release, two city officials interviewed in the film died, reviving the legend of the Livermore curse.

THE LIGHT FANTASTIC
Livermore

It's not often that a light bulb becomes the center of attention. Almost never, in fact, except in the case of one low-watt bulb with extraordinary staying power in a Livermore fire station. The four-watt handblown bulb was turned on in 1901, and it's been glowing ever since, making it one heroic light.

The little light bulb that could.

More than a hundred years of luminescence have earned the bulb a deserved spot in the limelight. The *Guinness Book of World Records* and *Ripley's Believe It or Not* have recognized it as the longest burning bulb in history. That's pretty heady stuff for a bulb that gives off as much light as a wimpy candle.

Technically, the bulb's lighting streak isn't continuous, since it has endured power outages as well as two moves from its original location in a hose cart house. Since 1976 it's been suspended by a thick cord from the white ceiling of a firehouse, where it casts a faint orange blush. The bulb is hung next to a water pipe and a fluorescent lamp, which does the real lighting here. The bulb is presented more as a symbol of American ingenuity.

Testimonial letters are framed on a nearby wall, including one from U.S. president George W. Bush. The bulb's fame is a mixed blessing for fire department personnel. It has brought them worldwide attention but also the awesome responsibility of making sure the bulb doesn't go out on their watch.

Visitors are welcome during business hours to view the subtle radiance of its thin carbon filaments. If you can't make it to the station at 4550 East Avenue, you can check out a Web site devoted to the bulb at www.centennialbulb.org. The site features a bulb cam that updates the mighty light's picture every thirty seconds.

A TWISTED TRAIL TO THE TOP
Mill Valley

The Mt. Tamalpais Scenic Railroad became one of the best-known thrill rides as soon as it opened in 1896. The 8.5-mile trek to the terminus near the Tamalpais peak had so many turns that the attraction was deservedly nicknamed the "Crookedest Railroad in the World." Hundreds took the journey each day in open cars that steamed up the 2,571-foot mountain, treating passengers to glorious views along the way. After hopping off the

THE HORSE AND HUMAN RACE

*C*urt Riffle grew up riding horses and later turned to marathon running. He was pleasantly surprised when he discovered a little-known competition that combines both sports into one mad dash of hooves and running shoes.

The sport of Ride & Tie features running tag teams of one horse and two runners. The basic rule is that both humans can't ride the horse at the same time so they must take turns riding the horse and then running on foot along a cross-country course that's usually 20- to 40-miles long. The first team to cross the finish line wins.

Races start with a furious scramble of runners, riders, and horses jockeying for position on the trail. "It's like the Oklahoma land rush, if you can visualize that," Riffle says. Horse and rider go ahead a mile or two, then the rider gets off, ties the horse to an available tree and takes off running. When the second team member catches up to the horse, he or she climbs aboard and then rides to meet up with the first runner. Then there's another "tie" and exchange of rider and runner. Top teams complete a 25-mile course in about two and a half hours.

Riffle is past president of the competition's sponsoring group, the Ride and Tie Organization, which holds about two dozen races each year. The contests are mostly in Northern California, where interest in the sport has been strongest since the event was launched in 1971 as a promotion for Levi Strauss jeans.

Riffle has been competing for so long that his horse, Corky, has logged the most miles of any other Ride & Tie animal. Corky knows the event method so well that when he's tied during the race, he immediately begins looking back for the trailing runner, anxious to get going.

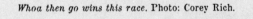

Whoa then go wins this race. Photo: Corey Rich.

A world championship is held each summer in a major destination, and spectators are welcome. Riffle says you may also be put to work helping to run the race if you want. For more information gallop over to *www.rideandtie.org* or phone (650) 949–2321.

train, visitors could enjoy nature walks, stunning vistas, and
dancing at a mountaintop pavilion.

The way down, however, was the most exciting part of the
adventure. The railroad company decided to put gravity to work,
sending passengers down the mountain in cars equipped only
with a braking device and a "Gravity Man" to operate it. The
brake was applied early and often on the one-hour journey down
through 281 turns at a 7 percent grade.

The railroad chugged along for a few decades, a popular
attraction on a mountain that had long fascinated locals. The
name Tamalpais comes from the Miwoks, and it means "Sleeping
Lady." In profile, the mountain looks like a woman with long hair
lying down for a rest.

The crooked railroad ran out of steam in the 1920s when a
road was built up the mountain and cars became the transportation of choice. It closed in 1930 after a fire damaged the track.

Now a group is trying to build a gravity-car barn that would
serve as an educational center and museum to tell the straight
story of the crooked railroad's history.

A REAL SWELL INVENTION
Oakland

A burning controversy in sports stems not from action on a
playing field but rather a feat in the stands. The debate concerns the creation of the wave, the stadium tradition where cas-
cading sections of spectators rise up, raise their arms, and then
sit down, generating the illusion of a rippling human wave. The
wave is now as common at ball games as the stadium hot dog,
and is a modern invention.

The most plausible claim to the wave's debut dates to a baseball
playoff game between the Oakland A's and the New York Yankees
at the Oakland Coliseum on October 15, 1981. That's when professional cheerleader Krazy George Henderson says he orchestrated

Did this man start the first fan wave?
Photo: Jon Terry.

the first wave around a stadium. It began slowly, he recalls. "I knew what I wanted, but no one had ever seen it before," he says. When it stalled, he encouraged fans to boo those who had let the wave die. Spectators finally mounted a robust wave that surged around the stadium. "It was great. The whole place just went nuts," Henderson says.

Henderson, known for his flopping mop of blond hair and trademark drum, says he first conceived of the idea as a student leading cheers at San Jose State University. He had done the wave at smaller venues before, but the 1981 A's game marked the wave's premiere at a professional sporting event.

Heated debate swirls around Henderson's claim, and frenzied exchanges have flared up on sports Web sites about the wave's provenance. The University of Washington has mounted a notable challenge, asserting that the first stadium wave originated during a Husky football game two weeks after Henderson's date.

Credible evidence appears to be on Henderson's side. In a 1984 newspaper interview, broadcaster Joe Garagiola, who was announcing the A's-Yankees game in 1981, recalled the wave happening when Henderson says it did. He marveled in the interview: "I had never seen anything like it before. It was super." Henderson's agent, Jon Terry, says he has received a tape of the game from Major League Baseball, and the wave is clearly evident during the broadcast.

Henderson is less sure about who came up with the name for the wave. "I have no idea," he admits. "Washington can take credit for that if they want."

A CRY-IN MOVIE THEATER
Oakland

New parents quickly discover the difficulty of resuming a normal social life once a baby arrives. If they want to leave the house with baby in tow, they have to lug several bags of supplies and then look forward to the icy stares in restaurants, theaters, and other public spaces if their child does the expected and lapses into a crying fit. It's no wonder that most parents remain housebound, where dinner and a movie means takeout and something on television.

Yes, there are sitters, but the Parkway Theater has something better: Monday-night shows geared to parents of babies one year and younger. We're talking first-run movies at an independent movie house that also features a pub that serves beer and wine and seating that includes comfy chairs and couches.

It's called the Baby Brigade, and the weekly program has been a screaming success since the theater debuted it in 1998. Shows routinely sell out. The appeal to parents is that they don't have to worry about a screaming baby disrupting anyone's enjoyment since plenty of babies are howling and everyone in the audience understands. There are mothers breast-feeding in the aisles and a line of parents at the back rocking fussy kids to sleep.

The Parkway is probably the first theater in the country to offer the service. One option before the Parkway's program was the soundproof crying rooms at some older theaters where parents could bring infants and watch a movie behind glass shields. But that only enhanced the feeling of being a social pariah for new parents. There are always drive-in theaters, too, but where are they anymore?

Other theaters have begun to follow the Parkway's lead. To check out the original program, drop by the theater at 1834 Park Boulevard on Monday nights, or get more information at the theater's Web site: www.picturepubpizza.com.

CARVING OUT A SPECIAL CAMPUS HANGOUT
Palo Alto

Stanford University students undoubtedly receive a distinctive educational experience, but those attending in 1994 had a truly special time. That's when ten artists from the South Pacific island nation of Papua New Guinea dropped by for several months to interact with the campus community and carve up some unique sculpture pieces.

The artists worked part of the day on their art. Then they par-
tied at night by putting on face- and bark-painting demonstrations and showcasing their drumming skills.

Giant logs of native hardwoods were shipped from New Guinea
to the Stanford campus for the project. The artists used sharp
adzes to shape the logs into totems and freestanding pieces that
include figures of alligators, people, birds, and fish.

Stanford is also home to a sculpture garden featuring the works
of Auguste Rodin. Apparently, the New Guinea artists weren't
daunted by the presence of competing sculptures by the French
master. Two of the works created by the New Guinea artists are
interpretations of Rodin's *The Thinker* and *The Gates of Hell*.

The artists eventually left, but their works remain in what is a
popular campus setting, the Papua New Guinea Sculpture Garden,
located at the corner of Santa Teresa Street and Lomita Drive.

AN OFF-KEY MARCHING BAND OUT TO PULL YOUR LEG
Palo Alto

Most school marching bands drill endlessly in their quest to
perform carefully synchronized halftime shows. Then there
are so-called scatter or scramble bands, which abhor traditional
formations and instead favor screwy, feverish rushes accompa-
nied by much yelling and helter-skelter movements. They are out
for parody, not precision, and none more so than the Leland Stanford Junior University Marching Band, the country's most notorious scramble band.

Stanford's band has constantly pushed the barriers of civility
during its infamous routines. A 1990 themed show at the University of Oregon lampooned a sensitive controversy between loggers
and environmentalists and featured whirring chainsaws and a
formation that projected a dead spotted owl. In 1997 the band presented a parody of the Irish potato famine during a game against

Notre Dame that was widely criticized. The band showed up at O.J. Simpson's murder trial in Los Angeles in 1994 and sere-naded prospective jurors, a performance labeled as a "new low in tasteless behavior" by Simpson's lead attorney, Robert Shapiro.

The group's mascot typifies the band's unconventional approach. It's a tree, and a pretty goofy-looking one at that. It's meant to represent the El Palo Alto pine tree pictured on school and city logos. For the band, it's the ultimate antimascot.

The tree's taunting behavior has landed it in some hot water, most notably involving confrontations with archrival University of California at Berkeley. During a basketball game at Stanford's Maples Pavilion in 1995, in fact, the tree exchanged wooden blows with Cal's Oski the Bear mascot, a skirmish that was widely replayed on sports shows around the country. In a football game the following year against Cal, the tree was roughed up by some students and had its branches clipped.

It was during a football contest against Cal in a 1982 Big Game that the band had its most humiliating moment. That's when they paraded onto the field in a premature victory celebra-tion, only to get caught off guard as Cal used five laterals to score as time ran out, with the winning Cal touchdown coming as the player with the ball unceremoniously knocked the band's trombone player right on his horn section.

More often, though, it's the Stanford band that delivers the blow that leaves others flat on their backs.

A Protocol for Politeness
Palo Alto

Democracy in action is sometimes not pretty, or at least civil. That's what happens, anyway, when you invite diverse opin-ions and let them play out, say, in a city council meeting.

Members of the Palo Alto City Council, weary of the con-tentious behavior that had reared its vulgar presence at recent meetings, decided in 2003 to draft a lesson in polite civics.

Call it a manners manifesto. The council's proposed code of conduct, however, apparently went too far in its quest to promote good behavior. Critics, and there were many, said the regulation would have outlawed common ways to convey frustration, such as scowls, sneers, and any other "nonverbal methods of expressing disagreement or disgust."

The proposed code was reported around the world, promoting global head-scratching and assorted mockery. Palo Alto became known as the town that frowned upon frowning. A few weeks later, with scores of reporters on hand to record every tic and glare, the council approved the code of conduct but took out the offending prohibitions. With the whole world watching, the council was all smiles when members nodded their heads in agreement to record the unanimous vote that preserved each member's right to be rude.

Afterward, council members, suitably chastened by the whole affair, admitted that the code had been too extreme as originally worded. In the end, they backed off from legislating manners when they realized that the First Amendment protects all forms of expression, even eye-rolling.

MANY GOT STUFFED BEFORE HEADING TO THIS RESTAURANT
Rio Vista

William Foster was a bootlegger on the run when he settled in this town in 1931 and opened a restaurant. Aside from illegal booze, his passion was big-game hunting. He made eight trips to Africa and about a dozen other hunting treks to Canada and Alaska. Apparently he was a good shot because he brought back loads of stuffed heads and carcasses from his travels.

His hunting trophies ended up being mounted on the walls of Foster's Bighorn restaurant, which offers good burgers and a chance to gawk at one of the world's most remarkable wild-game

You'll never drink alone here.

collections. It features the heads and sometimes the bodies of more than 300 wild animals from around the world. Underneath these mounts are photographs and detailed descriptions of Foster's hunting ventures.

Customers can sip a cold one in the bar or munch on steaks or cheeseburgers in the dining area under the eerily watchful gaze of an assortment of stuffed creatures, including moose, zebras, rhinos, apes, deer, elk, walrus, many exotic cats, and even a giraffe. The prize trophy is the mounted 13-foot-long head of a full-grown African elephant, with two 110-pound tusks and a face in a full-throttle roar.

Foster died in 1963, and Howard Lamothe now owns the restaurant. "I always say the mounts are on the wall, and the animals are at the bar," he says jokingly about his clientele.

If you don't like eating with anyone looking over your shoulder, this place isn't for you. For the rest head on over to 143 Main Street or take a virtual tour at www.fostersbighorn.com.

ONE WAYWARD WHALE

*H*umans have long admired the majestic migrations of whales and how these pods of ocean giants are seemingly guided by secret songs and mysterious sensory clues. Then there was Humphrey, a humpback whale with the directional sense of Mr. Magoo.

You see, when Humphrey's herd was making its annual autumn journey from Alaska to warmer waters off Mexico in 1985, Humphrey turned left at San Francisco when he should have veered to the right. Like a true male, he never stopped to ask directions and just kept right on swimming in the wrong direction, heading under the Golden Gate Bridge.

This whale needed a map.

He continued under several bridges during his impulsive tour of the San Francisco Bay area, heading in a northeasterly manner until he finally stopped about 40 miles up the Sacramento River Delta in shallow freshwater. There he paused to consider his next move.

By this time is was mid-October, and Humphrey's wrong turn was big news. Thousands of people a day began pouring into the town of Rio Vista to catch a glimpse of the hopelessly lost leviathan. Or was he really just an independent sort, out for a little sightseeing?

Scientists, concerned that the delta's freshwater environment could kill Humphrey, frantically tried many tricks to coax him back to sea. They played beckoning whale songs downstream and broadcasted sounds of an enemy killer whale upstream, hoping to get him moving in the right direction. After about a month he finally made the right move and eventually completed his migration.

Whale watchers continued to track his movements each year, seeking out his distinctive markings and observing whether he was going to march to his own current or stay with his herd. Sure enough, Humphrey made another wrong turn in 1988 and swam more than a mile into Bodega Bay north of San Francisco before heading back to sea.

Now, whenever a whale gets lost during migration, it is said to be making a "Humphreyesque" journey. Rio Vista has erected a marble marker as a tribute to Humphrey at the end of Main Street overlooking the river, a reminder that some wrong turns can lead to enduring fame.

THE SPOILS OF ROTTEN WRITING
San Jose

Writing poorly isn't very difficult. In fact, it comes quite naturally to some unfortunate scribes. A lack of clarity, wordiness, or ungrammatical sentence construction is routine work for lowly hacks. Crafting really putrid prose, however, the kind that makes readers wince and gag and howl with laughter, requires talent. That's why so many good writers compete in San Jose State University's annual bad-fiction writing contest. To be judged truly bad in this case means you must be pretty good.

The university's contest asks for the worst opening line to a potentially dreadful novel. It's called the Edward George Bulwer-Lytton Fiction Contest. You may not recall Victorian writer Bulwer-Lytton, but you are likely to know one unforgettable sentence he penned in his 1830 novel *Paul Clifford*. That book begins: "It was a dark and stormy night." That hackneyed phrase, often borrowed by the frustrated writer Snoopy to launch his writing career, has come to represent all that is wrong with bad writing.

The university's mocking tribute to Bulwer-Lytton has grown steadily since it was started in 1982 by English professor Scott Rice. Hundreds of writers wrack their brains to conjure up an opening assemblage of words that is so utterly bad it's actually good, or at least entertaining in its awfulness. There's an overall winner and also several categories of awards.

Contest rules are pretty simple. Each submission should be one sentence long and can be sent in by e-mail or regular mail. The address for entries is: Bulwer-Lytton Fiction Contest, Department of English, San Jose State University, San Jose, CA 95192-0090. You can learn more, and also get some good laughs reading past winning submissions, by visiting the contest's Web site at www.bulwer-lytton.com.

MUMMY DEAREST
San Jose

The 1972 Neiman-Marcus holiday catalog offered two Egyptian sarcophagi, intended as his-and-her gift items for "people who have everything." The Rosicrucian Egyptian Museum bought them, a purchase that made some sense. Although the folks there don't have everything, they do have 4,000 Egyptian relics, making the museum the largest collection of authentic Egyptian artifacts on display in western North America.

Museum director Julie Scott says they paid about $20,000 for the two coffins, and that price has turned out to be quite a bargain. As the sarcophagi were being delivered, workers discovered that a mummy was inside one of them, and what a mummy he's turned out to be. Museum officials continue to be surprised as they learn more about their acquisition, who is certainly no mere department store mummy.

Mummy is always here for you. Photo: Rosicrucian Egyptian Museum.

They originally believed the ancient corpse was a high priest known as Usermontu. An X-ray examination revealed a mysterious screw in Usermontu's knee, which they initially assumed had been inserted in modern times. But in 1996 three orthopedists removed the screw and were startled to discover that it was actually thousands of years old and remarkably similar in design to ones used in modern orthopedic surgery to reattach limbs. One significant difference was that Usermontu's knee surgery was most likely done after he died to prepare him for burial and the afterlife. News of a sophisticated surgical technique traced back to ancient Egypt created a sensation in scientific circles and garnered much publicity for the museum.

Now, Scott says, there's evidence Usermontu might be an even more significant find. In fact, he's probably not even Usermontu, and may be one of the missing Ramses pharaohs, she says. That makes him a star attraction at the museum, which has five other mummies and scores of other artifacts that detail ancient Egyptian life, including a popular walk-through rock tomb.

The museum also offers lectures and other special programs. To glimpse Usermontu, or whoever he is, visit the museum at 1342 Naglee Avenue or get more information and view artifacts online at www.egyptianmuseum.org.

SHE WAS UNDER THE GUN TO FIX THIS HOUSE
San Jose

Lots of home owners have remodeling horror stories. None can top the experience of Sarah Winchester, who began a fix-it job on her house in 1884 that lasted thirty-eight years and ate up most of her $20 million fortune. She couldn't blame project overruns on a bad contractor. At fault here was peculiar advice Winchester received from a spiritual medium who told her that she could ward off evil forces by never ending construction on her house.

This place is big enough for its own zip code.
Photo: Winchester Mystery House.

Winchester, heir to the Winchester rifle fortune, believed the seer when she told her that she was cursed because of all the death caused by the "Gun that Won the West." Fearing for her life, Winchester ordered carpenters and assorted contractors to toil away twenty-four hours a day until she died in 1922. The resulting chaotic design includes such oddities as stairways that lead to the ceiling, doors that open unto blank walls, and a cabinet that is actually a passageway to a section of the house. Winchester apparently also communed with spirits for ideas about home design.

When the last nail was hammered into place, the rambling residence contained 160 rooms, 10,000 windows, 47 fireplaces, and 2,000 doors. It has a few attractive amenities such as Tiffany stained-glass windows, working elevators, and button-operated gas lighting.

The incoherent abode is now a popular tourist attraction known as the Winchester Mystery House. There are guided tours by well-trained docents who have spent some time learning the home's curious floor plan. An adjacent Firearms Museum showcases the rifle that caused so much of Sarah Winchester's consternation. On Halloween and every Friday the 13th, there are flashlight tours for those who want to experience the home's haunted side in a spooky low-light setting. The home sprawls out at 525 South Winchester Boulevard. Information is available by calling (408) 247–2000 or visiting on the Web at www.winchester mysteryhouse.com.

POETIC PEARLS FROM AN UNLIKELY SOURCE
Sunnyvale

Junk electronic mail, known as spam, is a scourge of the digital age. Visitors to a unique Web site created by software engineer Allen Hutchison experience a more enlightened interaction with spam e-mail. Hutchison was plagued by hundreds of advertising come-ons ranging from the salacious to the sublime that clogged up his in-box daily and took precious time to wade through and delete. So he created a software program that would turn his spam into poetry. The program uses words in the headers of spam e-mails and creates a new haiku every fifteen minutes. It's then duly posted on his Web site.

He says creating the spam haikus, which he calls spamkus, has been an interesting diversion, and one that earned him fifteen minutes of Internet fame in 2002 when he got press coverage about his spamkus. "When attention peaked, I was getting 30,000 hits a day. People were happy that somebody found something interesting to do with spam," he says.

You can make so many things with spam, even poetry.
Photo: Jenna Hutchison

Here's an example of a spamku: "Homes for sale / from burn baby burn faster and / better with nero." Or another one: "Unclaimed Planes / trains and automobiles / will a war against."

Hutchison has generated hundreds of these poems on his site, an experience that's revealed some of the obvious qualities of spam, including that there's loads of adult-themed material.

Hutchison plans to upgrade his haiku program so that it doesn't create poems with numbers, but he wants to find a way to retain all misspellings. Apparently, misspelled words come up a lot in spam. "Words that are misspelled add a certain nuance to the poetry," he says.

Yes, you too can make spamku at home, because Hutchison provides a link to his program code for people to download. Or just sit back and read by surfing over to www.hutchison.org /allen/spamku.

NORTH COAST AND WINE COUNTRY

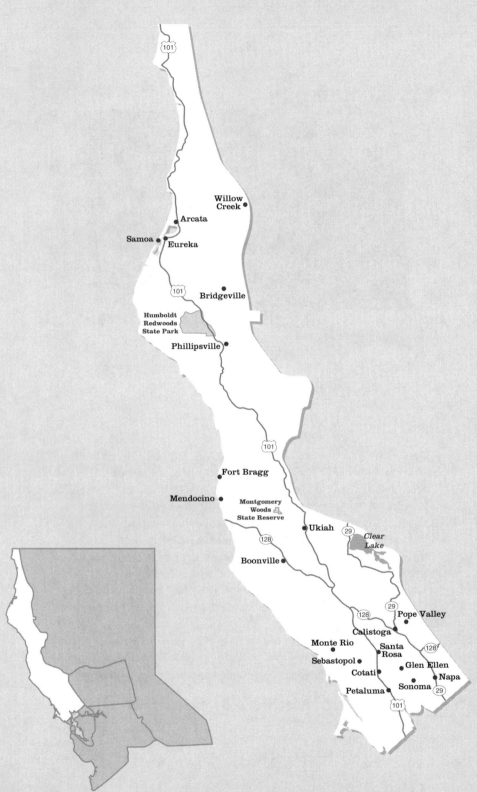

North Coast and Wine Country

A POETIC SPIN ON PROSAIC MISDEEDS
Arcata

Kevin Hoover's reporting may have some journalism professors cringing, but he's done something that no other newspaper writer has by making the usually dreary police blotter a must-read literary sensation. Hoover elevates the petty to the poetic by turning common offenses logged by the police into a literate and witty section of his weekly *Arcata Eye,* which he began publishing in 1995.

Sometimes he sticks to clever prose, but he even composes limericks and haiku and the occasional pop tune spoof. In the hands of lesser scribes, a report of a humdrum theft would be a snooze-inducing few lines hardly worth scanning. But just read Hoover's version of one such trivial act from 1998:

> On Valley East, trouble arose
> And evil's dark face was exposed
> When thieves, hearts gone hard
> Went into a yard
> And ripped off a guy's garden hose.

There's not much major crime here in this old logging town of about 16,000. Most of Hoover's musings concern reports of public disturbances, sometimes by local panhandlers, colorfully referred to by Hoover as "sidewalk socialites" or "leisure specialists."

About 3,000 locals subscribe to the paper, while thousands log on from around the world to the paper's Web site just to read its police log.

Hoover was drawn here by one of the town's more infamous acts of vandalism in the mid-1980s when someone stuffed cheese up the nose of the statue of President William McKinley. Hoover read the story and thought that a town with such antics would make a fun place to live and start a newspaper. Now it's Hoover who writes about further affronts to the statue. It's a local tradition for some prankster to slip a surprise costume on it every April Fools' Day. In 2003 Hoover reported in the *Eye* that someone had broken off one of McKinley's thumbs, referring to it as the case of the "disappeared digit."

Journalism instructors at Humboldt State University in town have gone on record as saying they wish Hoover would stick to the facts. For Hoover, facts are just a jumping-off point for his unique literary perspective on local sins, earning him the title of Master of Rhymes and Misdemeanors. You can see for yourself by logging on to www.arcataeye.com.

IF YOU DRIFT INTO THIS TOWN, YOU MIGHT NOT CATCH ITS DRIFT
Boonville

Out-of-towners might not grasp the hidden meaning behind the name of this town's Horn of Zeese Cafe. Unless, of course, they speak Boontling. Horn of Zeese means a cup of coffee in this obscure regional jargon first developed by Anderson Valley residents in 1880 and still spoken here. You see, a long time ago there was this guy named Z.C. who liked to make a strong cup of coffee, so residents named coffee after him. Get it?

That's how much of this quirky language grew, peaking in the early 1920s with about 1,000 words and phrases and 3,000 unique nicknames for inhabitants. In this isolated community,

That means a cup of joe to everyone else.

where privacy was scarce, Boonville residents had to be careful. Onetime transgressions might lead to an unflattering Boontling nickname that would haunt you the rest of your life. The term here for a feud is *haines-crispin,* named after former residents Haines and Crispin, who battled to the death over a property line dispute. Other names are more mundane, such as a Buckey Walter, the local term for phone booth. That came about because Walter was the first guy in town to get a phone, and the old five-cent pay call was made with an Indian head coin known here as a *buck.* Words sometimes derived from what they sound like, such as *keloppity,* which means to ride a horse.

The name of the language comes from the combination of clipped versions of Boonville and *lingo,* hence *Boontling.* Some linguists say it's the most extraordinary example in the world of a homemade language. They theorize that the language was developed as a secret code, perhaps as a way to allow adults to safely talk about sensitive matters in front of youngsters. Linguist Charles Adams collected all the Boontling terms in a book, which is fortunate because the language is dying out. Some old-time resident want it that way, preferring that it pass on with them. But if you visit town you're apt to still hear someone harpin' the old Boontling.

THIS TOWN WAS ALMOST VIRTUALLY GONE
Bridgeville

S hoppers on eBay accustomed to bidding on everything from used cameras to baby cribs got a shot at a much bigger prize in 2002. That's when the lonesome community of Bridgeville drew worldwide attention and ignited a mouse-clicking frenzy when it became the first whole town ever offered for sale by the popular online auction house. "It can be a private retreat, basking in the glory of the redwoods . . . or with proper development, Bridgeville can become an economic powerhouse . . ." the ad gushed.

The town's residents, all twenty of them, raised their eyebrows at this glowing description, knowing that their community had fallen on hard times in recent years.

The town had a restaurant, but it wasn't operating. Bridgeville's assets did include eighty-two acres of land, eight homes, a cemetery, streetlights, and a backhoe. That last bit of equipment, the eBay ad noted, would come in handy, since most of the structures in town were in a "fixer-upper" condition. On the plus side, however, the successful bidder would be the new proud owner of his or her own zip code: 95526.

The eBay ad languished at first, but worldwide news coverage of the virtual sale ignited interest, and hundreds of eBay customers started clicking in with bids, swayed by the vision of being king of their own California community. Eventually a winner emerged, identified only as a West Coast developer, who pledged a staggering $1.8 million, well above the $775,000 asking price.

More sober-minded locals thought the sale price sounded too good to be true, and it was. The buyer soon backed down, as did other eBay bidders, and the virtual auction fizzled.

Eventually the town was back up for sale in 2004 the old-fashioned way—with a traditional listing from a real estate office—and in May sold for $700,000.

EXPLOSIONS YOU CAN SET YOUR WATCH BY
Calistoga

An eruption implies spontaneity, which makes the geyser here most exceptional because it blows its stack like clockwork. There are only a handful of geysers that burst with such regularity that they've earned the right to be called Old Faithful. You may know America's more celebrated one in Yellowstone National Park. Calistoga is home to the only other Old Faithful in the United States.

Geysers erupt when a build-up of underground pressure generated by steam and heat break through surface rock. Geysers aren't normally punctual, but Calistoga's Old Faithful explodes every forty minutes or so, making it a viable tourist attraction. Visitors stroll into a dirt lot ringed by bamboo and tall pampas grass. They gather around shaded picnic tables and chairs to stare expectantly at a tiny pool with a few surface boulders. In between bursts the mood is languid here, with some people even dozing. Wisps of steam and the occasional hiss from the pond prompt people to grab their cameras and scurry into position. Some people aren't sure of how close they should get to the pond. After all, we're talking exploding steam here. There are many false alarms before it's finally showtime. Then the geyser shoots a spectacular plume of scalding water 60 feet into the air, maintaining it for a few minutes before receding back to its resting condition.

This irregular fountain has regular outbursts.

Olga Kolbek opened the attraction in 1973, closely monitoring the frequency of the geyser's daily bursts. She soon discovered that the geyser was a useful predictor of earthquakes. If the geyser's rate of eruption slowed, a quake was on the way, she found out. A further indication of an impending temblor was that the geyser would lose steam and only send up short bursts called "splits." Scientists dismissed her theory as a lot of hot air until Kolbek forecast the 1989 Loma Prieta shaker. Seismologists finally took notice and now keep a close eye on Kolbek's geyser for clues to earthquake activity.

Calistoga's Old Faithful offers a most unlikely companion attraction: fainting goats. Kolbek thought the goats, which topple over when startled due to a muscle condition, might enjoy grazing in the shadow of an erupting geyser. Go figure. For more information visit www.oldfaithfulgeyser.com or call (707) 942–6463. The geyser blows its top at 1299 Tubbs Lane.

A TIP OF THE SLONGUE
Calistoga

S am Brannan was clear about his vision to create a resort town in this Napa Valley region. He just wasn't as lucid about what it should be called. At a dedication ceremony in 1885, an apparently tipsy Brannan made Calistoga the only town in the world named after a drunken mispronunciation.

Legend has it that during a promotional party for the new town, Brannan, a businessman with an affinity for the sauce, was sufficiently juiced by the time he stood to address the crowd. His intention was to declare the new town the "Saratoga of California," modeled after Saratoga Hot Springs in New York. What Brannan unfortunately uttered in his inebriated exuberance was: "I will make this place the Calistoga of Sarafornia."

This town's founding father had a few too many.

Give the reporters on hand credit for accuracy, because Calistoga is the name that stuck.

Brannan had a clear vision for Calistoga's potential as a spa town. He was the first person to mix the area's thermal mineral water with volcanic soil from nearby Mount St. Helena, creating the restorative mud baths that makes Calistoga a major tourist draw.

After a soothing treatment some visitors stroll over to the town's oldest restaurant, where owners Drake and Madeline Dierkhising pay tribute to Brannan's fumbling moment by calling their place Cafe Sarafornia. "Everyone in town gets it," says Drake of his restaurant's unusual name. "But visitors come here and ask, 'Who's Sara?'"

SQUEEZING BACK INTO THE SPOTLIGHT
Cotati

The accordion has been called a lot of things, including the Stomach Steinway, Belly Baldwin, and the Waistline Wurlitzer. Yes, it's been labeled everything but hip.

The accordion does have its ardent followers, some who wistfully recall the glory days of the instrument in America, a popularity that peaked in the 1950s, when an accordion player with a repertoire of tunes could really get a party started. Then came rock and the accordion became decidedly uncool, drowned out by myriad riffs from electric guitars. It didn't help that the biggest name associated with the accordion was Lawrence Welk, not exactly a blazing figure to excite a new generation of accordion lovers.

True, the accordion mounted a surprising comeback in the 1990s, but let's not get hysterical. It has no chance of blowing away the guitar or even the bassoon for that matter in terms of being in fashion. But if the accordion is for you, the place to be once a year is Cotati, which has a lively tribute to the squeeze box that clearly demonstrates that it's a more versatile instrument than just a purveyor of polkas. In fact, the accordion is used in many cultures and styles of music, including zydeco, Cajun, mariachi, and even jazz, all performed during the two-day festival, a tradition since 1991. A popular moment in the weekend gathering is the Lady of Spain-a-ring, when everyone present with an accordion gets to blast this anthem in gleeful unison.

For more information, click on over to www.Cotatifest.com. An old bumper sticker emblematic of the accordion's lowly status said "Use an Accordion, Go to Jail." The Cotati festival has a new twist on that slogan as the event's theme: "Use an Accordion, Go to Cotati."

LAWN ORNAMENTS HOME DEPOT DOESN'T CARRY
Eureka

Romano Gabriel had a reputation in this town of being somewhat of a recluse. He reached out to others, however, in a rather unique way, constructing whimsical wooden figures using a hand-saw and placing them on his front lawn for passersby to enjoy.

Gabriel, a carpenter who came to the United States in 1913, arrived in Eureka and began crafting hundreds of brightly colored and fanciful figures out of discarded wooden vegetable crates. He put them up in his small yard behind a picket fence. These figures included dozens of faces with heavy dark eyebrows and red lips, with some featuring an odd assortment of examples of bad hair days. These faces project expressions of surprise or incipient smiles. Gabriel also carved and painted flowers and other brightly colored patterns on artworks that eventually took over his front yard and obscured the view of his home.

Not surprisingly, his artwork attracted many tourists, and
Gabriel often hid in back to watch the many people come and
admire his creations. He died in 1977, but a local effort succeeded
in preserving his works, which are now housed in a downtown
storefront for viewing at 314 Second Street, watched over by the
Eureka Heritage Society.

M ILLING A BOUT IN THE P AST
E u r e k a

If you drop by to watch Eric Hollenbeck at work, and he encour-
ages you to do so, you might find him toiling away at a pedal-
powered scroll saw from the early 1900s. Other days he and other
workers at his wood mill might be crafting a Victorian-style
architectural design on a machine made in the Victorian era. The
most modern piece of equipment at Hollenbeck's Blue Ox Millworks was made in 1948. Most of it dates from 1866 to 1910.

Don't feel bad that Hollenbeck hasn't modernized his tools. He
wouldn't have it any other way. He created the mill in 1973 as a
throwback to his early days of logging and working on timber
survey crews. He discovered old mill machinery scattered in
nearby woods that had been abandoned by companies long out of
business. Over the years Hollenbeck taught himself to use the
equipment, and now he has an authentic Victorian mill that
attracts hundreds of visitors a year.

Visitors can step back in time and watch workers in the blacksmith shop, where tools and machinery are made by hand. There
are also vintage print and ceramics shops, as well as the mill,
which turns out custom-made architectural pieces for Victorian
homes. Hollenbeck has also restored a skid camp, a unique exam-

The older the better at this factory.
Photo: Cudahy Studios.

ple of an old logging camp with a cook shack, bunkhouse, and theater. Skid camps were put on sleds and hauled to new areas in the early days of logging.

The Millworks is also a unique high school that enrolls several students each year to pursue traditional studies that are integrated with the mill's schedule. For example, students learn science and math by completing various projects at the mill. There are also classes for adults, including basic blacksmithing, for those looking to forge a new career. For more information call (707) 444–3437 or visit them online at www.blueoxmill.com.

MOBILE MOBILES

*I*f you've ever wondered how a big banana might fare
against a giant duck in a bicycle race, the Kinetic Sculpture
Race has the answer. The truth is that neither would give
Lance Armstrong a run for his money. But crossing the finish
line first isn't the main point anyway of this race. It's the sheer
brazen wackiness and the creative excess, not to mention the
human folly of trying to coax rolling artworks along a gruel-
ing 38-mile course.

The idea for the race began in 1969 when Ferndale artist
Hobart Brown put his creative talents to work on his son's tri-
cycle, adding some artistic flourishes and two extra wheels. He
was challenged to a race through downtown Ferndale by others who built equally zany contraptions. The winner that year
was a 10-foot-long turtle on wheels built by a local metal
sculptor.

The race has grown in popularity and participation. It's
now an annual three-day marathon Memorial Day weekend
featuring dozens of sculptures on wheels navigating a tricky
land and water course. All entered sculptures must be powered
by people, meaning they are pedaled, paddled, and sometimes
prodded and shoved along. There are lots of prizes, including
the Aurea Mediocritas, awarded to the competitor deemed the
most average. The wheeled artworks, shaped like colossal
fruits, animals, and more abstract designs, are rolled through
streets, waterways, and beaches from Arcata to Ferndale.
Recent entrants have included a giant chocolate éclair and an
85-foot salmon.

This is one quacky race.
Photo: Humboldt Kinetic Association.

Brown has helped start other kinetic races around the world, including Australia and Poland, and in several U.S. cities, including Baltimore. Kinetic races have been called the triathlon of the art world. So far, no one's called them dull.

Pedal over to www.kineticsculpturerace.org for more information or call (707) 845–1717. If you're in town but miss the race, you can head over to Ferndale's Kinetic Sculpture Museum at 580 Main Street and view entrants from past races.

YOU COULD SMELL THIS TRAIN A-COMIN'
Fort Bragg

Folks in Mendocino County didn't need to hear a whistle blowing to know that the Fort Bragg to Willits train was approaching. Chugging along ahead of this locomotive was a windblown stench that announced the train's imminent arrival. So foul was the odor that locals nicknamed it the Skunk Train, and the putrid moniker clung like, well, a train to a track.

This train once caused a big stink.

Photo: Christopher Hart.

The Skunk Train began operating in 1885 as a lumber transport. The smell of the train's gasoline engine, combined with the malodorous wafting from onboard pot-bellied stoves used to keep passengers warm, created the telltale aroma that gave the Skunk its name and infamy.

A nickname like Skunk is usually unpleasant baggage to carry around, but it hasn't been a heavy burden for this train. The Skunk evolved nicely from its early lumber days into a popular tourist train with a sweeter-smelling engine. The Skunk offered one sweet trip through beautiful terrain that included a stretch alongside the Noyo River and into redwood forests. Thousands took the 40-mile journey each year for a round-trip that left from Fort Bragg. The Skunk also kept up its postal duties, making it the longest-running train in America to make daily mail deliveries.

The Skunk shut down in 2003 for financial reasons but was taken over by a new company that revived the service the following year. Climbing onboard was Chris Hart of Sierra Railroad, who proudly called himself president of the Skunk Train. He's thinking of turning the Skunk into one hot place for entertainment, including the possibility of onboard dining and theater-style entertainment. The future looks rosy for the Skunk. To keep track check out www.skunktrain.com.

GEMS OF THE TRASH HEAP
Fort Bragg

Glass Beach wasn't always shown much respect. In fact, locals turned it into the town dump. For about twenty years, beginning in 1949, Fort Bragg residents had a rather unique way of taking out their trash: They simply hauled it to the area's rugged coastline and dumped it off a cliff into the raging surf below. Whatever it was, from household rubbish to rusty old cars, off it went. This didn't end until the late 1960s when common sense finally took hold.

Beachcombers here find jewels and junk.

From an environmental standpoint, using the ocean as a garbage dump was a disaster. But the shortsighted plan had unexpectedly pleasant results in the long run. Nature literally turned some of the trash into treasure. Through the years the pounding surf smoothed and polished thousands of pieces of glass into colorful and shiny gems that litter the beach, giving it its name. Beachcombers willing to sift through the occasional rusty spark plug or car wheel scoop up dozens of these rainbow-hued glass pebbles as souvenirs. Another common sight here are scurrying shellfish such as crabs, obviously grateful that the beach's days as a dump are in the past.

About 40 miles south, in the small town of Point Arena, nature has crafted another unique beach. Bowling Ball Beach gets its name from prehistoric boulders lining the beach that have been finely ground by the surf through the years. At certain tide levels the smoothly rounded boulders appear like rows of giant bowling balls lined up on the sand. It's a favorite with photographers.

JACK LONDON'S GREAT MYSTERY STORY
Glen Ellen

Jack London was one of America's greatest storytellers, and his own life was just as dramatic and intriguing as anything he set down on paper. The prolific author of such classics as Sea Wolf and *Call of the Wild* was also known as a social activist, farmer, sailor, and adventurer. He lived his last years in Glen Ellen, where he owned a sprawling ranch with his second wife, Charmian.

Jack London's home was all hearth.

In a tragic twist worthy of one of London's own tales, a majestic palace of redwood and stone that London spent years planning and building mysteriously burned to the ground just days before he and Charmian were set to move in.

London's Wolf House was a monumental four-story dwelling that featured a fifty-seat dining room, a "stag party" room, indoor reflecting pool, sleeping tower, and several fireplaces. After construction began in 1911, London declared that the house would stand for "a thousand years." Instead it burned to its stone foundation in 1913 as finishing touches were being applied. Arson was suspected, but nothing ever proven. London died three years later at age forty, never having lived in his dream house.

In 1995 a team of ten expert fire investigators spent four days sifting through the charred remains and concluded that although arson could not be ruled out, the most likely cause of the disastrous blaze was the spontaneous combustion of rags soaked with linseed oil that had been used the day of the fire to finish woodwork in the dining room.

You too can sift through the Wolf House remains, or at least peer in at the ghostly ruins of the stone foundation, by hiking to them on the grounds of the Jack London State Historic Park at 2400 London Ranch Road.

For a glimpse of more misfortune for London, check out some of the more than 600 rejection letters he received during his long writing career. They're on display in a house built after his death by Charmian and dedicated as a museum about Jack London after her death in 1955. This London abode has the mirthful name of a survivor: The House of Happy Walls. For more information, call (707) 938-5216.

THESE SPIRITED GUESTS NEVER CHECK OUT
Mendocino

With its foreboding ambiance, the Mendocino Hotel is an obvious locale for ghost sightings. In fact, spirits are just another hotel amenity, drifting about amid a Victorian setting that includes dark oak furnishings, stained-glass windows, brass fixtures, and antique oil portraits glaring down from the papered walls. That charm quickly wears off if you have a ghostly

Waiter, there's a ghost in my chair.

encounter, though. One screaming guest scampered to the reception desk in the middle of the night and pleaded with a hotel clerk for an immediate change of rooms to escape a ghoul disturbing his sleep. Room 216 appears to be a phantom hot spot.

There's not much safety in the public spaces here, either. A woman haunts tables six and eight in the dining room, a dimly lit corner with several mirrors. Another ghostly presence hangs out in the lobby, staring out at the sea with a forlorn look as if waiting for someone to return. Late at night clerks have noticed buttons on an adding machine mysteriously moving by themselves. Other hotel workers have been startled by overhead lamp cords swinging wildly in rooms with no detectable breeze.

The hotel has worthy credentials for poltergeist activity. The main part of the building dates to 1878, when it opened as the Temperance Hotel, aiming to be an oasis of Christian virtue amid a booming logging town supporting dozens of saloons and brothels. The seaside town's climate, with its creeping fog, provides an ideal backdrop for mischievous spirits.

If you dare, visit the hotel at 45080 Main Street or phone (707) 937–0511. You can visit online at www.mendocinohotel.com.

VEGETABLES FROM AN OCEAN GARDEN
Mendocino County

John Lewallen has long been an ardent promoter of a food source that most Americans consider nothing more than an unsightly beach nuisance. It's seaweed. Yes, those tangled piles swarming with flies that dot most sandy recreational areas. Most of us would rather kick it away with disgust than put it in our mouths to savor.

Seaweed has found its way into kitchens around the world, most notably in Japan. Lewallen was an American oddball in the late 1970s when he arrived in the Mendocino area looking for a

Seaweed sandwich, anyone?
Photo: Barbara Stephens.

new career and thought he might have found one harvesting seaweed and selling it to health-food stores.

He began by trial and error, ripping out chunks of the stuff
from the surf and nibbling on it. Sometimes a stomachache
resulted. "There are some really bad-tasting ones, some 'yuck, forget it' ones," he says of the thousands of seaweed species out
there. But there are a few that make edible sense, and by 1980 he
founded the Mendocino Sea Vegetable Company and began offering about a dozen varieties for sale. "There's still an intense deep
prejudice," he says of eating seaweed in America. But consumers
have turned to it for health reasons, as many varieties are rich in
minerals and vitamins. And now gourmet chefs are including it
on their menus, using it for soups, sushi rolls, salads, teas,
breads, and even desserts.

Lewallen works hardest in June and July, harvest season for seaweed when it's in bloom. He takes what he needs and hauls it back to his home in the Anderson Valley to dry and bag for sale. A few competitors have sprung up along the coast here, making this one of the biggest seaweed-harvesting regions in the country. So far, they've all remained friends, meeting in the late spring for a ceremonial opening of the season.

Lewallen doesn't see the seaweed market ever exploding in America, but he thinks it will remain popular with a niche following, especially for those who have their favorite types. For example, he says, "The sea palm is one groovy noodle."

For more information contact the company at (707) 895–2996 or visit its Web site at www.seaweed.net.

Encampment for the Elite
Monte Rio

President Herbert Hoover once called the annual summer gathering here of Bohemian Club members the "Greatest Men's Party on Earth." The atmosphere at times rivals a frat house keg party, according to reports, but there's also some highbrow political hobnobbing that transpires as well. Oh, and also boating, musical performances, plays, lakeside chats, games of dominoes, and the consumption of lots of wine and spirits.

Local news reporters formed the San Francisco club in 1872, but soon they were banned as the men's club grew more exclusive and private. Club members began heading to this Russian River community in 1879 as a way to unwind, and it's been an annual event ever since for political bigwigs, policy honchos, industry captains, and other prominent people including scientists, doctors, and artists. Every Republican president since Calvin Coolidge has attended.

The event begins with a ceremonial burning of a mascot named Care, to symbolize liberation from everyday concerns. There are skits and lectures and lots of outdoor recreation on the club's 2,700-acre property that includes a major redwood grove. Conspiracy theorists have alleged more-sinister robed rituals take place, but nothing has ever been proven. However, some major political deals have been consummated here, most likely over a strong drink or two. At the 1967 camp Ronald Reagan reached agreement with Richard Nixon to stay out of the upcoming presidential race, and other reports say that the Manhattan Project got its start at a meeting during World War II.

The elitist nature of the event and the fact that major policy decisions are sometimes made here behind closed doors has led to opposition. Most years a local protest group lines up to wave signs and shout slogans at the arriving guests, an event that has become just another one of the retreat's rituals.

Food for Thought
Napa

A re potato chips just a good-tasting salty snack to you? Or do you sometimes hold a chip in your greasy fingers and contemplate just what makes them so yummy? Better yet, have you ever thought about what a potato chip means to American culture?

At Copia, the American Center for Wine, Food & the Arts, food is much more than pure sustenance. It's something for your brain to munch on as well. The unique museum offers exhibits, seminars, and other programs that explore the significance of food in America and the role of cuisine in defining culture and heritage. And yes, an examination of the potato chip was one of the scheduled offerings here.

If all that's a little highbrow for some, you can just eat your way through the place and let the goods bypass your brain and head directly to your stomach, no questions asked. That can be done by scooping up samples at some of the museum's special cooking demonstrations or by dining at its signature eating spot,

Julia's Kitchen, named for Julia Child, described by the museum as the patron saint of the pantry.

Others may want to digest some of the exhibits here, including the core show *Forks in the Road,* which offers several interactive stations that encourage people to play with food and give it some thought. At one station you can guess the intended use of mystery kitchen gadgets. You can also listen to classic food songs, examine the sometimes strange language of short-order cooks, and test your sense of smell.

Some of the exhibits center on the art of making food. Others, such as *Return Engagement,* display artworks made from discarded food containers and old kitchen devices. The surrounding gardens are a destination, too, with tours offered that demonstrate the uses of a wide range of herbs, fruits, and vegetables.

This boy's learning some common scents.
Photo: Copia.

The museum is located at 500 First Street and can be reached by calling (707) 259–1600. If you'd like to work up an appetite for the place first, visit the center online at www.copia.org.

A CASE OF MUSTARD MANIA

Mustard is your basic condiment, most often squeezed over a ballpark frank for added flavor. In Napa Valley for two months out of the year, mustard is much more than that. It takes center stage on the plate, no longer just a lowly yellow paste to be dripped over a main dish but the central course itself. That's the basis for the annual Napa Valley Mustard Festival.

The impetus for the festival, organizers say, are the wild mustard blooms that sprout and carpet the valley in hues of green and gold during late winter. Cynics have said it's just a clever way to draw visitors to the tourist-hungry region during a traditional slow period from January though March. But Poupon to them.

The festival is serious business for some, including premium-mustard makers who compete for the coveted award of all-around best mustard. The top mustard is chosen from a surprising array of categories, including coarse grained, pepper hot, herb, American yellow, exotic, and even fruit mustard. At judging events you're apt to see tasters relishing and contemplating a dab of mustard on their palate as if it were a drop of some of the area's most precious wine.

For the rest of us the event features lots of yellow-themed fun, including a marketplace with a bounty of mustards to sample as well as food, drink, and entertainment. Related cultural happenings during the period include concerts and art exhibits. All in all, this is a celebration that really cuts the mustard. For more information on tickets and an event schedule, check out www.mustardfestival.org.

Award-winning mustard chefs are all smiles.
Photo: Napa Valley Mustard Festival.

A CALL TO ARMS WRESTLING
Petaluma

B ill Soberanes gave a leg up to arm wrestling, elevating it from its lowly barroom-brawling status to an internationally recognized sport, with a little help from Snoopy along the way. Soberanes, a local newspaper columnist who called himself "Mr. Petaluma," began promoting arm wrestling contests at the town's Gilardi's saloon in 1952. With Soberanes pumping it up, the competition grew into the World Wristwrestling Championship.

Snoopy got the arm wrestling bug in a series of *Peanuts* comic strips that ran in 1968, which helped promote the sport and Petaluma's big event, although it didn't do much for Snoopy. In the strip he's disqualified in the finals because he can't lock thumbs with his opponent as required by the rules—because, alas, beagles don't have thumbs.

The *Peanuts* series prompted ABC's *Wide World of Sports* to televise the Petaluma championships for the next fifteen years, driving its popularity up and bringing it worldwide attention.

When he wasn't grabbing people's arms, Soberanes was taking their picture, or posing for a picture with somebody famous. He claimed that he had been photographed with more celebrities than anyone in the world. He had the pictures to prove it, too—hundreds of them. In a 1972 photo, Soberanes is seen arm wrestling with Ronald Reagan, then governor of California. The future president not only beat Soberanes, he also broke one of his ribs. Soberanes always maintained the Reagan had cheated by starting before he was ready.

In 2003, the year Soberanes died, it was announced that the Wristwrestling Championship would move out of town after a fifty-year run in Petaluma.

Aarggh!

Petaluma paid tribute to Soberanes with one of the most intense civic monuments you're apt to find. It features the twisted torsos of two straining arm wrestlers in midgrip, veins popping and faces frozen in contortions of pain and determination, forever locked in a battle that will never be decided. For a peak at this grimacing pair in bronze, head to the corner of Petaluma Boulevard and Washington Street.

A Drive Through the Woods, Literally

Driving into a tree can be disastrous. But driving through one can be marvelous. There's no better place in the world to try it than the North Coast, which has more drive-through trees than any other region in the world. It's home to several stands of colossal redwoods, considered the world's oldest and tallest living things.

The Mendocino Tree in the Montgomery Woods State Reserve near Ukiah, for example, is believed to be the tallest living thing at 367½ feet. The Rockefeller Forest in Humboldt Redwoods State Park is considered the world's largest remaining stand of redwood trees.

All this lumber first drew loggers, who quickly harvested 95 percent of the redwood groves in Northern California. If it weren't for chainsaws, most redwoods would live well over 2,000 years. Those that remain here are a major tourist draw. North Coast visitors seeking a spiritual connection with these majestic forests also embrace a slew of quirky roadside attractions that have sprouted up in the shadow of these magnificent trees.

In addition to drive-through trees in Myers Flat, Leggett, and Klamath, there are also tourist draws such as the One-Log House 8 miles south of Garberville on Highway 101 (707–247–3717), a kind of oversize motor home made from one redwood log that was more than 2,000 years old.

The Trees of Mystery at 15500 Highway 101 in Klamath (800–638–3389) boasts a talking giant statue of Paul Bunyan and a silent but equally massive Blue Ox, as well as gondola rides through a redwood forest. There's also a trail that leads to unusual-shaped trees such as the cathedral specimen, which is nine trees in one. Couples can be wed here, humbled by the knowledge that no matter how strong their marriage is, it would never outlast the tree they stood under when they exchanged their vows.

No burgers or fries at this
drive-thru in Leggett.

A COMPANY THAT'S STICKING AROUND
Petaluma

Andrea Grossman's idea to market a line of decorative stickers started as a small home business as she worked from her dining room table and employed her twelve-year-old son, Jason. Her opening set of a dozen stickers launched a sticker craze in the early 1980s, and Grossman's concept of a small company became unglued. In fact, Grossman, a graphic artist, ended up creating the largest sticker operation in the world, Mrs. Grossman's Paper Company. With printing presses rolling twenty-four hours a day,

Stick around awhile.

Photo: Mrs. Grossman's Paper Company.

the company produces more than 15,000 miles of stickers each year. If you were so inclined, you could place each sticker it produces on the ground and make it halfway around the world.

The stickers range from colored letters of the alphabet to more elaborate patterns and pictures of animals. Most people affix them to greeting cards or scrapbooks.

The company plant, on a bird preserve, has an unusual policy regarding pets. Employees are allowed to stick with their dogs during the day and bring them to work, and many do. Touring visitors usually encounter several of the pooches wandering about. They can also marvel at the massive printing presses churning out the more than 700 different stickers the company produces, a far cry from its humble beginning in 1979.

To relive the early days of stickers, visit the plant's Sticker Museum, which has vintage designs on display. Visitors can also try their hand at creating a postcard with stickers at the end of the tour. For more information call (800) 429–4549 or stop by 3810 Cypress Drive. You can also stick close to the company's Web site at www.mrsgrossmans.com.

A LWAYS R EADY FOR ITS C LOSE - UP
Petaluma

When director George Lucas needed a location to serve as the backdrop for *American Graffiti,* a classic view of small-town American life in 1962, he cast Petaluma. In fact, Petaluma often gets the call when Hollywood is looking for a time-warp setting evocative of early Americana. Production crews hardly have to touch a thing in town before the cameras can roll, as Petaluma is naturally a throwback community with picturesque Victorian homes and stately downtown buildings. Films from *Peggy Sue Got Married* to *Howard the Duck* have been shot here, as well as numerous commercial and advertising spots.

This town has a long list of film credits.

Before Hollywood came calling, Petaluma earned recognition
with some unusual civic claims, including being the home of the
world's first and only chicken pharmacy. That made sense, since
the town was once known as the World's Egg Basket because of
its substantial poultry industry from the 1880s through 1940.
The town celebrates that status with an annual Butter and Eggs
Days celebration every spring. Call (707) 763–0344 for more
information.

Petaluma also stakes its claim as being the takeoff point for
the nation's first airmail flight in 1911. Pilot Fred Wiseman flew
to nearby Santa Rosa to deliver three letters and several dozen
newspapers. There's no record of whether any eggs were onboard.

L*ORD* *OF* *THE* T*REE* R*INGS*
Phillipsville

I n this land of tall trees and kitschy roadside stops, the Chimney
Tree coffee shop already had a strong enough draw to lure travelers in the form of a massive tree hollow spacious enough to
serve as an apartment. In 1975 the Redwood Highway attraction
added a unique feature to really make it stand out: a half-mile scenic trail decorated with colorful dioramas re-creating scenes and
depicting life-size characters from J.R.R. Tolkien's *The Hobbit*.

The trail here is charming enough, with redwoods and a
stream, but it is the hobbit scenes that elevate the hike to another

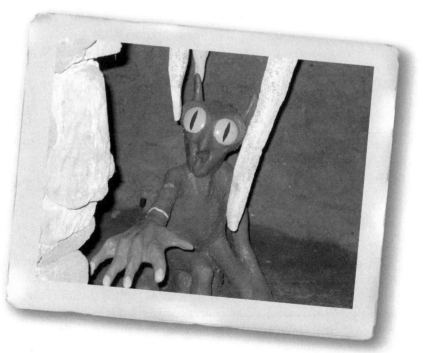

No, I'm not E.T.

level. Visitors are taken into the Land of Middle Earth, beginning with a scene of the hobbit shire and a towering wizard Gandolf paying a visit to Bilbo Baggins, who is shown relaxing on a hillside smoking a pipe. Further along the trail there are scenes of Baggins killing a large spider, elves being chased up a tree by howling wolves, and a lime-green gollum cowering in a rock hollow who looks a lot like an alien. At certain spots visitors can push a button and hear a British-accented male voice describe the action being depicted in the woods.

The attraction is called Hobbiton. Tami Satterlee says it was opened by her grandmother, Peggy, who loved Tolkien's books. The success of the movie version of the *Lord of the Rings* trilogy has helped Tami in that more people finally know about hobbits. "Before," she says, "we'd have to explain how a hobbit was a creature with fur on its feet." The popularity of the movies hasn't boosted visitors to Hobbiton. Most people come, she says, to view the Chimney Tree, which stands over 78 feet tall. It has a burned-out hollow you can enter that is a room with a diameter of 12½ feet. The center of the tree was burned out in a 1914 fire.

Others also stop by for the great burgers and homemade pies. You'll find it all at 1111 Avenue of the Giants. Hobbiton can be reached at (707) 923–2265.

CAPPING A LIFETIME ACHIEVEMENT
Pope Valley

This rural community is mostly known for its annual turkey shoot fund-raiser and a unique folk art display that elevates the humble hubcap to a loftier level of contemplation. Pope Valley's most famous resident was Emanuele "Litto" Damonte. He spent three decades collecting and then artfully exhibiting hundreds of hubcaps at his ranch, earning the appropriate title of King of the Hubcaps.

That's one way to decorate a fence.

From the road, visitors spot shiny chrome wheel covers dangling from a fence. On the property they are attached to walls, trees, and the side of a barn. They are on walls inside the barn, too. In all, about 2,000 hubcaps form this sprawling piece of environmental art. There are also other recycled car parts on display, as well as metallic stars, bottles, and pulltops. Some of these items are arranged to spell out Damonte's nickname, Litto.

Damonte died in 1985, and soon after his ranch was declared a state historic landmark. A plaque at the site calls it "one of California's exceptional 20th century folk art environments." While he was alive, Damonte received help with donations from friends and neighbors. Now visitors can help out, too, and be a part of this unique artwork. Just drop off a hubcap, if you can spare one, at 6654 Pope Valley Road.

A TASTE OF LOGGING HISTORY
Samoa

In the early days of logging, the cookhouse was no doubt a lively place. Not only did it serve as a social hub for a mill's workforce, it also was the scene of daily battles by cooks and waitresses to satisfy the voracious appetite of hard-working lumberjacks, who toiled twelve-hour days, six days a week. Loggers were served three hot meals daily at a cookhouse where the tables were long, portions were grand, and manners were in short supply. Attitudes were gruff at mealtimes until men had their fill of heaping plates of meat, vegetables, bread, and pie. With full stomachs, the loggers turned more sanguine about returning to work.

For a taste of that bygone lifestyle, visitors can stop at the Samoa Cookhouse, the last remaining logging camp cookhouse in North America. It opened in 1893, but in recent years it's been turned into a public restaurant. Diners may not know how to work like a lumberjack, but here they can experience what it's like to eat like one. Forget about your romantic dinner. Everyone here sits "family-style" at long cloth-covered tables as mounds of food are offered up just like in the old days, when no one was turned away hungry. As you stagger away from the table, you might want to wander over to the nearby museum, which includes historical photographs of area logging operations and the cookhouse. That should help get the digestion process started.

Not surprisingly, the Samoa Cookhouse caters to large parties and tour groups. For more information, phone (707) 442–1659. To get there cross the Samoa Bridge from Eureka and turn left, then follow the signs.

Leave your table manners at the door.
Photo: Samoa Cookhouse.

GOOD GRIEF—A MUSEUM?
Santa Rosa

A comic strip hardly seems the stuff to base a museum upon. But *Peanuts* was no ordinary strip, and its creator, Charles Schulz, no common cartoonist. During the peak of Schulz's fifty-year-run with *Peanuts,* the strip starring Snoopy and Charlie Brown appeared in hundreds of newspapers and was enjoyed by more than 350 million readers.

Still, Schulz initially resisted plans for a museum, downplaying all the fuss and acting more like Charlie Brown than Charles Schulz. But he eventually relented and the Charles M. Schulz Museum and Research Center opened in 2002 here, not far from his home and the studio where he created much of his work.

The two-story structure keeps the fun stuff downstairs with rotating exhibits of some of his original strips. There are also permanent exhibits including *Morphing Snoopy,* a 7,000-pound wood sculpture by Japanese artist Yoshiteru Otani that features forty-three layers that are cut away to show the evolving appearance of Snoopy from Spike, Schulz's boyhood pet, into the beagle made famous by the strip. Another prize here is a wall of art recovered from a Colorado home where Schulz once lived and covered with early drawings of his *Peanuts* characters in 1951. The artwork had been covered up with four coats of paint by new owners, then restored and donated to the museum.

Visitors upstairs can examine Schulz's drafting table and other memorabilia from his life, including personal papers, books, and photographs. There's also a classroom where budding cartoonists can come and practice their stuff.

Schulz admired the environmental artist Christo and mentioned him in a 1978 strip, with Snoopy wondering whether the artist's next project would be to wrap his doghouse. In a case of

Here's to you, Charlie Brown.
Photo: Rick Samuels.

life imitating a cartoon imitating life, Christo came to the museum in 2003 and completed Snoopy's wish. He presented the museum with a doghouse covered in tarp, polyethylene, and ropes. It's appropriately entitled, *Wrapped Snoopy House.*

The museum is located at 2301 Hardies Lane and can be reached at (707) 579-4452. Its Web site is at www.schulz museum.org.

A HARD TRADITION TO BRING BACK
Sebastopol

A few generations ago most Americans knew that an apple a day wasn't only good for keeping the doctor away. It could also be crushed to make a fermented beverage with a nice kick that would help take the load off a difficult day. Hard cider was flowing freely as far back as colonial times in America, mostly because apples were plentiful and making cider was relatively cheap and easy. Even second president John Adams, a leader of the American Revolution, wouldn't face the day without consuming a daily tankard of apple cider with breakfast, allegedly to calm his stomach.

America's cider tradition died out with Prohibition, but it's making a comeback in the twenty-first century, helped in part by British native Jeffrey House, who in 1999 opened America's first cider pub near Sebastopol. "There's nothing more American than apple pie, and cider is just liquid apple pie," House observes.

In an area dominated by grape vines and wineries, people sometimes overlook that there are plenty of apples being grown in the Sebastopol region. In fact, it's one of the top apple-growing areas in the country. The cider produced for House's Ace-in-the-Hole pub is made mostly from the local Gravenstein crop, though he tosses in some Granny Smiths for added tartness, plus a secret yeast that House says produces a high-quality cider.

"There's nothing too difficult in making cider. If you let apple juice sit out long enough, it will go alcoholic," he says. House says he employs a more complex process to control flavors that makes his cider mill more like a wine-making operation.

Visitors sit in the shadow of the attached cider mill in a patio and bar area made mostly from redwood recycled from an old water tower. The pub offers hard cider such as regular apple, pear, berry, honey, and other seasonal varieties. To get to the core of this place, visit 3100 Gravenstein Highway or surf over to www.acecider.com.

A GARDEN MONARCHY
Sebastopol

Louise Hallberg likes to keep butterfly cocoons in her bath-room. They're not for decoration. Actually, it's for their pro-tection. She finds them in her garden and brings them inside; otherwise those pesky spiders will eat them. It's just one of the things Hallberg does to keep a watch over her prized butterfly garden, a sanctuary for about three dozen species of butterflies, including monarchs.

The gardens surrounding her house have been a personal sanc-tuary, too. She's lived in the same dwelling since she was born in 1917. When she was a little girl, her parents planted some pipevine plants, which are vital to the life cycle of the pipevine swallowtail butterfly. Each year several dozen of them make an appearance in her garden. She begins looking for the chrysalises of those and others in the spring, scooping them up and bringing them inside for shelter until they are ready to hatch into adult butterflies and be released into her garden.

The many fluttering insects make Hallberg's garden a prime visiting spot, especially with schoolchildren. Every week busloads stop by to wander among the flowers and the butterflies, though she can never guarantee what they'll see. Sometimes fog or chilly air will limit the show. But if the weather's right, many butter-flies will be spotted quivering about from spring through fall. Hallberg loves showing people around, so call her at (707) 823–3420 to make an appointment for a tour.

FAST AND FABULOUS

*M*artin Swig has a vintage car collection worthy of a museum. But these aren't mere showpieces. Swig often takes them on long rides through Northern California, a place with lots of scenic highways and back roads and plenty of stops for gourmet grub. "It's a nice confluence of factors that makes it one of the greatest places for driving in North America," Swig says. Every year dozens of other vintage car enthusiasts come along for the ride in an event organized in 1990 by Swig known as the California Mille.

Swig based his tour on a historic Italian road competition known as the Mille Miglia, first held in 1927. It was a thrilling 1,000-mile annual rally through Italy that eventually was stopped in 1957 when cars became so fast the event turned deadly for drivers and spectators. When the Italian race was revived in the 1980s, Swig got the idea to import a swankier version of it to California. It's more a premiere social event than gritty road rally. The 1,000-mile excursion begins at the posh Fairmont Hotel in San Francisco, where everyone can gawk at the entered roadsters, which need to be of vintage 1957 or older. Most are vintage jewels of the road such as Jaguars, Masseratis, and Aston-Martins, some worth over a million dollars. These aged racers roar over the asphalt, attracting crowds along the Northern California tour that takes four days to weave through parts of the Mendocino coast and Napa Valley. Entry fees for the exclusive event are approaching $5,000, and the race is limited to sixty vehicles.

The elitist nature of the tour spawned a parody event, the California Melee, which was limited to cars built before 1973 of no historical significance. Swig showed he had a sense of

A 1957 Mercedes-Benz on the California Mille.
Photo: Martin Swig.

humor by organizing another race mocking his own Mille, the Double 500 Motor Tour, limited to old cars costing no more than $500. This is now another annual event that goes from Marin County to Ukiah and back—if the entered clunkers can make it that far.

For more information on the California Mille or Double 500 races, speed over to http://californiamille.com.

A BUDDING GENIUS
Sebastopol

To Luther Burbank, a rose was never just a rose, or a walnut never just a walnut. Fruits, nuts, vegetables, and flowers were raw materials for Burbank to recast in myriad and sometimes fanciful ways. Burbank's experiments with plant breeding began with the humble potato. After he arrived in California in the 1880s, he launched a far-reaching experimental farm here that at its peak had him testing millions of strains of new fruits, flowers, and vegetables.

Burbank wasn't aiming to produce a freakish fruit show. His primary interest was to retrain plants for better production to increase the world's food supply.

By the time he died in 1926, Burbank had introduced 800 new varieties of plants, including more than 100 different plums and prunes, 10 types of apples, the Shasta daisy, and the freestone peach. No one believed you could cross an apricot with a plum until Burbank succeeded, giving the world a new fruit called the plumcot, now a produce staple.

Burbank successfully bred more new plant varieties than any other person in American history. It's no wonder that California honors him by celebrating Arbor Day on his birthday, March 7.

Burbank's Gold Ridge Experiment Farm is open year-round for self-guided or docent tours, so you can see the fruits of his labors, including the Paradox walnut tree, a hybrid of the English and California black walnut, which Burbank created more for the quality of its lumber than the appeal of its fruit. The farm is at 7781 Bodega Avenue in Sebastopol.

His historic home in nearby Santa Rosa, where he often entertained celebrities of the day such as Thomas Edison and Henry Ford, is also open to the public. It's located at the intersection of Santa Rosa and Sonoma Avenues and can be reached by calling (707) 524-5445.

SWINE OR URSINE?
Sonoma

The grizzly bear blazoned on California's state flag is fierce and bold, an appropriate symbol for a populace that values its intrepid spirit. In its original form, however, the dynamic bear was more like a flaccid pig. The bear design adopted as California's official state flag in 1911 was based on the banner of the Bear Flag Republic, the hastily hatched and incredibly short-lived domain of 1846. That flag was raised in Sonoma on June 14 when

A replica of the original bear flag.
You decide about the bear.

a small band of American settlers led by John C. Fremont surprised themselves and Mexican general Guadaloupe Vallejo after
storming his fort. Vallejo was literally caught napping. He offered
the Americans some wine and his unconditional surrender.

Fremont and his men declared the region the California Republic, and a first order of business was raising a suitable flag to
rally around. Reports say that a nephew of Mary Todd Lincoln,
William Todd, painted the republic's banner using material from a
women's petticoat. The flag featured a five-pointed star as a tribute to the lone star of Texas, the words "California Republic," and
a red stripe across the bottom. Todd also included the shape of a
grizzly bear, an important icon of intimidation and force appropriate for a newly crowned republic in a region teeming with hos-
tile enemies. The only problem was that many observers
snickered that the flag's bear looked more like a pig than a dominant animal to be feared. Native Americans who saw it, historians
say, muttered the word for pig as they gazed at the republic's flag
flapping in the breeze.

Of course, calling it the Pig Flag Republic doesn't have quite
the same cachet as the Bear Flag Republic, which is how this ter-
ritory is referred to in historical texts. The republic didn't last
long, however. In less than a month, the United States claimed
California and the American flag was raised at the fort. The Bear
Flag Republic was over. The original banner was burned during
the San Francisco earthquake of 1906. A replica of the original
flag is displayed at the Sonoma Barracks museum at 36 East
Spain Street at the town's downtown plaza. Call (707) 939–9420
for more information.

GOOD FOR WHAT ALES YOU
Ukiah

The terms *organic* and *brewpub* don't seem compatible. Imagine an organic eatery and you think herbal teas and tofu. A brewpub is all about burgers, fries, and boisterous customers quaffing sudsy liquids. The Ukiah Brewing Company smoothly blends these two concepts under one roof. It became the first federally certified organic brewpub in 2000 and only the second certified organic restaurant in the country.

Els and Allen Cooperidder, both biologists passionate about natural food preparation, opened the pub and restaurant in a historic downtown building after plowing through a mountain of paperwork to gain the cumbersome certification. They've also had their place certified organic by the state of California.

It wasn't easy. For example, they battled with health inspectors so they could use an environmentally-friendly cleanser made from hydrogen peroxide, rather than the mandated bleach inspectors were insisting on. They've also had to overcome perceptions by some customers that organic pub fare is bound to be boring. It's not. In fact, you can find saloon favorites here such as burgers, nachos, garlic fries, and bowls of chili in addition to more exotic items such as Flemish pot roast, Thai curry vegetables, and pan-fried Pacific oysters. There's a tasty lineup of brews featuring a dozen lagers, ales, and stouts made from organic grains and hops, plus organic wines from local vintners.

The pub has a saloon's traditional decor of brick and wood. There's live music on weekends, about the only thing here that's not certified organic. Even the salt and ketchup are all-natural. Hop on over to 102 South State Street for a taste or visit www.ukiahbrewingco.com for more information.

MAKING A BIG DEAL ABOUT A BIG FOOT
Willow Creek

R eported sightings of a giant man-ape in this neck of the woods haven't been flattering. A hairy, smelly, hulking creature almost 10 feet tall with an ungraceful saunter is the common description. Yet the folks of Willow Creek have embraced the ungainly being known as Bigfoot as if he were the sexiest hominid alive.

Willow Creek is proudly referred to as the gateway to Bigfoot country, with a decided wink toward tourist dollars. Local businesses have added the tall legend to their names, as in the Bigfoot Motel or Bigfoot Lumber. At the local cafe you can order the Bigfoot burger, a large patty of meat shaped like a foot.

The Willow Creek–China Flat Museum has a permanent wing dedicated to Bigfoot items, including a plaster cast of an alleged track made by Bigfoot in 1958 that started the whole Sasquatch craze. A road worker in nearby Six Rivers National Forest discovered the unusually large footprint, and word of the find began circulating in the press, leading to the appropriate nickname of Bigfoot to describe the elusive forest man-ape. More proof came in 1967 when a Bigfoot stalker shot a wobbly one-minute film that showed some kind of apelike giant moving through an area of downed trees. Some have called it a hoax, saying it's nothing more than a man in a monkey suit.

Reports of giant manlike brutes date back further than the Bigfoot legend here and are common to many cultures and continents. The Bigfoot of the Pacific Northwest has gained some believers in legitimate scientific circles, however, including primate expert Jane Goodall, who was scheduled to come to Willow

Step foot into the Bigfoot Museum.
Photo: Sue Doane.

Creek in 2003 when it hosted the International Bigfoot Symposium. In the end Goodall didn't make it, but about 200 others did to hear lectures such as one entitled "Apelike anatomical and behavioral characteristics of the Sasquatch."

Not everyone here believes in the Bigfoot legend, of course, but no one doubts that Bigfoot has given Willow Creek a leg up on the tourist trade. The museum can be reached at (530) 629–2653.

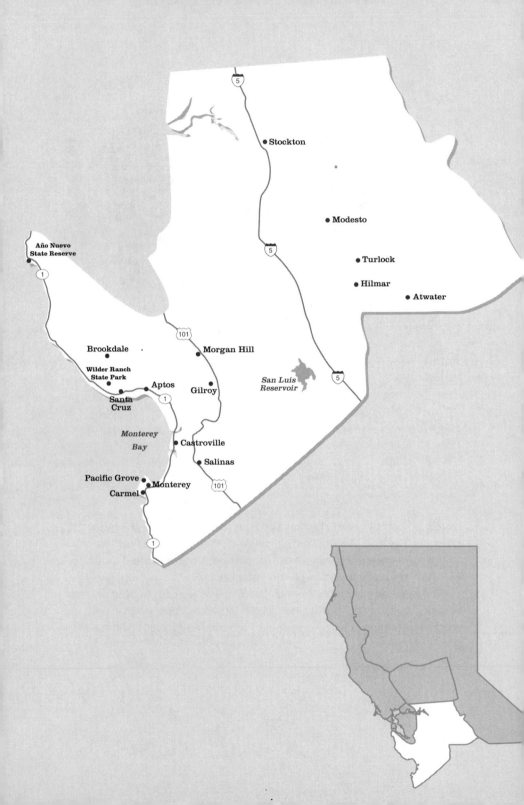

CENTRAL COAST AND VALLEY

Año Nuevo
State Reserve

• Stockton

• Modesto

• Turlock

• Hilmar

• Atwater

Brookdale

Wilder Ranch
State Park

Aptos

Morgan Hill

Gilroy

San Luis
Reservoir

Santa
Cruz

Monterey
Bay

Castroville

• Salinas

Pacific Grove

Monterey

Carmel

Central Coast and Valley

First Make War, Then Love
Año Nuevo State Reserve

The blubbery and often violent aspects of the elephant seal's sex life are on full display during the winter months at this windswept point and protected wildlife area north of Santa Cruz. In what is one of the world's most unusual spectacles, two-ton male elephant seals measuring up to 16 feet in length come ashore each December to battle it out for the right to mate with female harems. These sausage-shaped gladiators thump chests, bite, and struggle for dominance before an alpha emerges to claim his turf and make whoopee with dozens of females. All is not lost for the losers. Less brawny but perhaps more wily, they can sometimes sneak in a little nooky when the alpha isn't looking, or is just too tired to object. Meanwhile, other males simply frolic with logs on the beach out of frustration.

Guided tours of the reserve during the mating season are some of the hottest tickets around. In addition to witnessing the battle of the sexes between the males, visitors can also catch new pups nursing with mothers and taking their first uncertain swims in the ocean.

Behind all the wrestling-style mating is a true animal-protection success story. Elephant seals, named for the long schnozes of the males, once numbered in the hundreds of thousands before mass hunting of them in the 1800s nearly wiped them out. Protection

Where elephant seals get busy.

efforts by Mexico and the United States helped preserve the few remaining seals, and they began showing up at the reserve again in the 1960s. Now hundreds are born on the beach and in the sand dunes here each year, making this the world's largest mainland breeding colony for the elephant seal.

A visit in the summer is less visually exciting, as the seals return to hang around on the beach and molt. The most activity you're likely to see is when they move up the beach toward the end of the day to get a little warmer. For information on a visit, contact the reserve at (650) 879–2025.

A PARADE THAT NEVER REALLY GETS GOING
Aptos

It takes more time to dress for the Aptos Fourth of July Parade than to actually march in it. They prepare like crazy for the annual event, decorating floats, practicing dance moves, making costumes, and dressing up their pets. There's loads of anticipation awaiting the pageantry. The crowd lines up early. Then they go out and march for all of two blocks. A twirl or two of a baton, a few bars of music, a prance or two from a horse, and then it's all over and wait until next year.

Aptos bills its fleeting procession as the world's shortest parade. Since they've established a standard of two blocks long, it would be hard for any other town to mount a challenge to this title. Then again, a one-block parade is always an option.

What Aptos lacks in parade distance it makes up for in enthusiasm. Planners say that nearly everyone in town marches in it. And it seems that every dog does, too, with many in costume. There are horses, bagpipe players, floats making political statements, and lots of cars and trucks. It takes up to two hours for every marcher to make it through the abbreviated parade route along Soquel Drive.

A TOWN'S SOFT SPOT FOR A HARD-LUCK SHIP
Aptos

If you believe the exhibits at the visitor center at Seacliff State Beach, the dilapidated hull of crumbling concrete at the end of the pier here was once an able seagoing vessel. It's hard to fathom, though, because the wreckage of piled asphalt hardly resembles anything you might call seaworthy.

This is the USS *Palo Alto,* or what remains of it. Ill-fated hardly begins to describe this ship's downward spiral. The *Palo Alto* was constructed with much promise in Oakland in 1919 at a cost of $1.5 million, an oil tanker made out of cement because of a shortage of steel. It was designed for the war effort, but by the time it was finished, the ship was no longer needed and remained docked in San Francisco Bay for nearly ten years. The *Palo Alto* plunged in value and was sold for scrap and towed to Aptos, where a company made gala plans to launch it as a party ship. It appeared that the *Palo Alto*'s fortunes were destined to improve. The ship was permanently grounded in the bay and a pier built to reach it. It opened with great fanfare in 1930—right at the height of the Great Depression. Once again, the *Palo Alto*'s timing could not have been worse. Posters of the day promised "amusements galore" aboard the ship, which included a casino, dance hall, swimming pool, arcade, and carnival concessions. But within two years the party was over, sunk by the company's financial problems. A savage storm soon dealt it a vicious blow across the midsection. The *Palo Alto*'s demise was now assured.

Despite its ugly appearance, locals have developed a big heart for the *Palo Alto.* The ship was donated to the state in the 1960s and for many years used as a popular fishing pier. Now the relic is so damaged that the only living things allowed on it are birds and seals. But below the ship's surface its hull has become a thriving marine habitat, and so there are no plans to do away with it. On the contrary, every June the ship is feted with the Festival of the Cement Ship. Music and dancing from the 1930s are the main attraction, and many people come dressed up in period clothes. The mood is definitely buoyant, which is more than can be said about the ship the event honors.

GROUNDED FOR LIFE
Atwater

A visit to the Castle Air Museum is a thrilling if somewhat incongruous experience. In a pastoral setting more suited for a croquet tournament are nearly four-dozen vintage military aircraft, including some of the biggest and deadliest bombers ever flown and a sinister and speedy spy plane once used during the Cold War to sneak high-altitude peeks of the Soviet Union. The planes date from World War II through the Vietnam era and

A World War II and Korean War bomber at the
Castle Air Museum.

include bombers, fighters, spy planes, tankers, and cargo transports. These historic crafts have come to a final resting place in a grassy field covering eleven acres.

Visitors can wander about and ponder the immense size and former destructive powers of the B-52D Stratofortress, once the largest aircraft ever flown. It could deliver over a hundred 700-pound bombs, and it was so massive that it required wheels on its wings to land. Another big bomber, the B-29 Superfortress, displays Korean War–era bombing icons and artwork on its exterior. The SR-71 Blackbird displayed here could peer down upon enemy sites from 80,000 feet and is still ranked as the fastest-flying plane with speeds of up to 2,350 mph.

All the planes here have made their final descent. They've been lovingly and painstakingly restored by a crew of volunteers. Walking among these historic planes is a moving experience.

While the real treat here is gazing up at all the vintage war birds parked outside, there is an indoor museum as well with lots of war memorabilia. There's a restored cockpit from a Vietnam-era B-52, two WWII-era plane engines, and a display case with military artifacts from World War I. Some of the docents here are veterans who flew some of the craft on display, and they're just as much a resource as the exhibits. Fly over to the museum at 5050 Sante Fe Drive or visit online at www.elite.net/castle-air.

AND A BROOK RUNS THROUGH IT
Brookdale

The Brookdale Lodge takes rustic dining to a whole other level by featuring a babbling brook coursing right through the center of its restaurant. The seven-tier dining room is built right around a mountain stream lined with stone banks and featuring swimming trout. As impressive as it looks, the dining room with the enclosed waterway is not the historic inn's major attraction. Many visitors drop by hoping to be spooked by one of the lodge's many ghosts. In fact, the Brookdale Lodge is rumored to be haunted by no less than forty-nine restless spirits. When it comes to ghosts, this hotel can hang up a NO VACANCY sign.

The inn was built in 1900 and the unusual restaurant added in the 1920s. For a long time it was the haunt of a fast Hollywood crowd. Now it's just haunted. The most common sighting is that of a little girl named Sarah, the niece of the former owner who drowned in the restaurant's brook. She's seen and heard often, sometimes calling out for help. Sarah's got lots of company. Visitors wandering about have reported a cacophony of poltergeist noises, including phantom dinner parties and mysterious footsteps, as well as cold spots and eerie aromas. So far no one's spotted the ghost of President Herbert Hoover, who once stayed here during the inn's early heyday. Make a spirited visit to 11570 Highway 9, or visit online at www.brookdalelodge.com.

NOTHING ORDINARY ABOUT THESE ORDINANCES
Carmel

This former artist's colony sure looks pretty on the surface, but for decades it has been the site of fierce political battles over seemingly trivial concerns. Perhaps no other American burg can match Carmel's peculiar slate of proposed laws, or equal the amount of passion generated by each piece of quirky legislation.

It's no wonder that Clint Eastwood rode in on his high horse in 1986 to run for mayor and flash his best scowl in an effort to knock some sense into the City Council. After two terms he'd had enough and gave up on politics.

Let's examine the legislative record here to get some perspective. Carmel banned ice-cream cones in the 1980s, ostensibly because the dripping treats sullied sidewalks. Some suspect it was an effort to rid the town of take-out food places.

If you're wearing heels in this town, you'll need a permit.

Residents need city permission to prune trees, or they face fines. If you want to walk through town wearing high heels, you'd better have a permit or face a fine. It's not a fashion statement but a protection against high-heeled litigants who fall while walking on city property.

The city once waged a furious but half-baked debate over a proposal to legislate the mix of cookies and muffins a store could sell.

If you want to be charitable, at the heart of these zany civic debates is an understandable desire to preserve the town's quaint charms. This is a tourist town that doesn't really want to be a tourist town, at least if it means yielding to souvenir hawkers, T-shirt outlets, and chain stores.

Or maybe it's a sign that things here are just different. The downtown area known as Carmel-by-the-Sea is almost too charming with its gingerbread-style architecture, initiated in the 1920s by architect Hugh Comstock.

As further evidence of Carmel's unique style, residents resisted having street addresses for many years. Homes instead were known by cutesy names such as Tinkerbell, Teapot, Hansel, and even side-by-side residences known as This Is It and This Isn't. It drove emergency personnel and pizza deliverers nuts. Finally, some common sense prevailed in 2001 when the Carmel City Council, after much debate and a close vote, of course, approved home mail delivery and the inclusion of street addresses.

THIS TOWN HAS A CHOKE HOLD ON THIS VEGETABLE
Castroville

An artichoke doesn't exactly invite you to take a bite, at least not in the way that a juicy apple does. The artichoke is a complicated tangle of thorny and pointed leaves. It's an intimidating offering that requires a plan of action before you dig in. You gotta work to enjoy it.

Castroville has a big heart for the artichoke. The region of Monterey County produces almost all of America's artichoke crop. That's why Castroville is known as the Artichoke Capital of the World. If you need a visual clue, check out the massive sculpture of a giant artichoke outside the restaurant and fruit stand of the same name at 11241 Merritt Street. It's an overgrown, towering leafy ball that looks like a genetic experiment gone awry. The giant vegetable is actually made of cement and was constructed in 1972. It stands 20 feet high and 15 feet wide, and symbolizes just how big the artichoke really is in this town.

Each July Castroville celebrates the artichoke with a festival that includes a parade, games, crafts, and, of course, lots of arti-

Artichokes really are big in Castroville.

choke-themed fare. There's an artichoke-eating contest where entrants are given a plate with six artichokes and told to eat as many as they can in three minutes. Not exactly your average sporting event. As an interesting bit of trivia, festival organizers crowned Marilyn Monroe their queen in 1947, well before she launched a movie career. They know artichokes here, and they can also spot Hollywood talent. For more information on the artichoke festival, call (831) 633-2465.

Two other agricultural festivals of note also take place in this region. There's the Garlic Festival in Gilroy, held the last full weekend of July (408-842-1625), and the Asparagus Festival in Stockton, held the fourth weekend of April (800-350-1987). Just so no one goes nuts about feeling left out.

MAKING TREES DO TRICKS
Gilroy

Axel Erlandson was pretty intrigued when he discovered a natural graft between two sycamore trees. If nature could do it, so could he. Although many doubted him at first, including his wife, in the 1920s Erlandson began carefully shaping trees into ornamental patterns and shapes. Sometimes he combined several trees into one, or else he bent and trained one tree to grow into a fanciful figure. Before long he had a veritable nursery of freaks such as Zig-Zag, an American sycamore that looked like a lightning bolt, and Oil Well, three box elders shaped like an oil derrick.

Trick or tree?

In all Erlandson pruned his way to a collection of more than seventy oddly shaped trees, enough to open a roadside attraction near Santa Cruz in 1947 called the Circus Trees. He beckoned people to see the "World's Strangest Trees," and they certainly qualified. Included in the collection were the Basket Tree, six sycamores woven together to make a latticelike trunk, and another combination of two box elders shaped to look like a spiral staircase.

After Erlandson died in 1964 his Circus Trees languished, but they have been given new life in the unusual setting of an amusement park. Nineteen of Erlandson's Circus Trees eventually took root on the lush grounds of the Bonfante Gardens Family Theme Park, an amusement park with 10,000 trees, several gardens, and a few dozen kiddie rides and attractions. Owner Michael Bonfante, a food-store magnate and tree lover, brought the Circus Trees to his park and planted them throughout the grounds. In a way this agriculturally-themed park is the perfect place for the trees. As visitors stroll amid rides such as twirling garlic bulbs and the Mushroom Swing they can marvel at Erlandson's masterpieces, such as his oldest surviving work, the Four Legged Giant. The giant is four American sycamores that arch into a shared trunk more than 8 feet off the ground, giving off the appearance of a large, lumbering creature.

To see the trees, visit the park at 3050 Hecker Pass Highway or take a virtual tour at www.bonfantegardens.com.

WHEY, WHEY BIG
Hilmar

The Hilmar Cheese Company is a muenster of the cheese business. The company's claim of being the world's largest single-site cheese producer is as solid as one of its forty-pound blocks of cheddar. Hilmar says it produces a million pounds of cheese each day. If you don't believe them, they invite you to stop by and watch, certainly one of the more unique ways to spend an afternoon.

The Big Cheese.

Upstairs at the company's visitor center, you can peer down at
workers in lab coats and hard hats bustling about amid massive
stainless-steel equipment as they churn out mounds of cheese
curds that are piled high in huge steel carts. When you've had
your fill of that sight, you can move on to other interactive
exhibits, such as one where you can sniff the aroma of various
cow feed. With the scent of hay roughage still in your nostrils,
venture over to have a gander at Buttercup, a fake cow inside a
glass display case, where you can watch a simulation of the
plant's automated system of milking. If you're in the mood, grab
a device and feel the pulse of a milking cow. That's all upstairs.
On the first level, conveniently located near the gift shop and
cafe, you can watch a detailed, life-size diorama that explains how
cheese is made in such massive quantities here.

Hilmar may be the biggest cheese company you've never heard
of since they only sell their own label at the visitor center. But
they produce blocks and blocks of varieties such as cheddar, Monterey Jack, American, and Muenster that are sold to fast-food outlets and restaurants. To get a sense of the scale here, they sell
500-pound barrels of cheese to wholesale customers, or enough
cheese to make tuna melts into the next decade.

You can sample Hilmar's own cheese at the visitor center,
including an item they call Squeakers, a cute name for what is
really fresh cheese curds. They are more remarkable for the
whiny sound they make when you bite them than for their taste.

Hilmar officials have said they're in the "milk reconfiguration
business," which means they find many uses for the nine million
pounds of milk squeezed out of hundreds of local cows and delivered to them every day. Besides cheese, Hilmar makes about
350,000 pounds of whey protein and lactose powder every day,
most likely putting them at the top of the heap in those products
as well. To see what a big cheese really looks like, head over to
Hilmar's visitor center at 9001 North Lander Avenue. You can
take a virtual cheese tour at www.hilmarcheese.com.

INSTANT MINISTER
Modesto

You don't need a lot of religious training to be ordained a minister by the Universal Life Church. If fact, none at all. What you do need is a computer mouse, printer, and access to the Modesto-based church's Web site. Just by submitting your name on an online form, you receive a "pop-up credential" that you can print out and then, presto, you're a minister.

The ministry-by-mouse-click is just the latest trend for the Universal Life Church, which is probably the world's largest and most well-known religious organization offering instantaneous ordinations. The church has ordained more than twenty million ministers since it was founded in 1959 by Reverend Kirby Hensley in his garage in Modesto. He was brought up as a Baptist but opened the church on the doctrine of religious freedom. Protected by the First Amendment, he fought off legal challenges to the legitimacy of his church for decades until his death in 1999. The church has continued on and even picked up the pace of its ordinations though the Internet.

According to the church, ministers it ordains are legally able to perform weddings in all fifty states. They can also do baptisms and funerals. Those looking for more spiritual guidance can send away for supporting materials such as the "Minister-in-a-Box," which includes books and materials to start a ministry and then gear up for doing ceremonies. The church is nondenominational. In keeping with the principle of religious freedom the church is based upon, it doesn't charge a fee to be ordained. To visit the church online, go to www.ulc.org.

WHAT WOULD HEMINGWAY SAY?

*T*he sport of bullfighting, immortalized for its brutal glamour in Ernest Hemingway's Death in the Afternoon, gets the California treatment every summer in the Central Valley. You can call it bullfighting lite. It still isn't much fun for the bull, but, unlike similar events in Mexico and Spain, the bull gets to walk home after it's over. Of course, chances are he's headed to the slaughterhouse anyway, but that's another story.

The Central Valley is the nation's hotbed for bloodless bullfighting, thanks to the strong support of the Portuguese community here. Traditional bullfighting, which ends with the killing of the bull, is banned in the United States. But so-called bloodless bullfighting is legal in California as long as it happens in connection with traditional religious festivals as practiced by the Portuguese community. The action consists mostly of the teasing of the bull by matadors with red capes. Instead of real lances that pierce the bull's neck in traditional bullfighting, the bull here wears a Velcro patch on his shoulders and is stuck with Velcro-tipped spears by riders on horseback. It's embarrassing to the bull, but not really painful.

Bloodless bullfighting may also be a misleading term since injuries are still possible, but most likely to the human participants. In an event that has to be considered taking a metaphor too far, these bullfights feature teams of young men who enter the ring with the aim of literally grabbing the bull by the horns and wrestling it to a standstill. Although the bull's horns are shaved and covered with leather caps, these teams of bull grabbers are still thrashed about, sometimes leading to broken bones.

The bloodless bullfighting season is off and running in the Central Valley from May to October, with most of them happening during the summer. These events are associated with Portuguese celebrations of religious holidays and are a tradition brought to this country from their native home. They are considered important cultural and social events here, and are not widely publicized. You can find a link to the schedule by going online to www.bullfights.org. There are bullfights in towns such as Stevinson, Tulare, Tracy, and Gustine.

HISTORY LINKS AND RESTAURANT CHAINS
Monterey

The Cannery Row of John Steinbeck's stories was not a place of touristy shops and restaurants near a world-class aquarium, as it is today. As big a talent as Steinbeck was, he'd be hard-pressed to dredge up novel fodder from a visitor destination lined with T-shirt vendors, chain eateries, and trinket shops.

These old fisherman shacks are part of
Monterey's canned history.

The Monterey of John Steinbeck's era in the 1930s and 1940s was a place of atmosphere and colorful characters. In the 1945 novel *Cannery Row,* he called it "a poem, a stink, a grating noise, a quality of light, a nostalgia, a dream." Imagine saying that about another Bubba Gump Shrimp restaurant, a prime dining spot in modern Cannery Row. Steinbeck's works were more like journalism than fiction. "Doc," a recurring character in Steinbeck's Cannery Row stories, was based on his real-life pal Ed Ricketts, a Monterey marine biologist and philosophizer who first drew Steinbeck to the area.

You can discover some of Cannery Row's history if you veer off the beeline path most visitors take as they shuttle between the Monterey Bay Aquarium and the marketplace of shops and restaurants. Ed Ricketts's lab, for example, still stands at 800 Cannery Row, a weather-beaten wooden shack that most people pass without a glance. Across from Ricketts's lab is an often-overlooked historical exhibit of three fisherman shacks. You can peer into the windows and view the harsh living conditions they endured represented by the sparse furnishings, mostly tiny cots and tables with packs of cigarettes, coffee mugs, and newspapers.

Two other Steinbeck-related sites nearby include the La Ida Cafe, a bordello in Steinbeck's works but now a restaurant, and the Wing Chong Market next door, a former Chinese grocery and now an antiques shop.

A memorial to Ricketts stands at the corner of Drake Avenue and Wave Street. It's the intersection where Ricketts was killed when the Del Monte express train barreled into his stalled car in 1948.

The Cannery Row Foundation, a preservationist group, sometimes offers tours of historic Cannery Row. For a history lesson and more information, go to www.canneryrow.org or call them at (831) 372–8512. For a campier but still fact-filled journey, albeit in wax, visit the Spirit of Monterey Wax Museum at 700 Cannery Row (831–375–3770), which presents 400 years of Monterey history through several action-packed dioramas.

MR. WILSON WOULD HATE THIS PLACE
Monterey

Just one pint-size scamp living next door was enough to enrage the perpetually grumpy Mr. Wilson in the long-running newspaper comic *Dennis the Menace*. You can just picture his face turning red and steam rising from his ears if he happened upon the Dennis the Menace Playground, a sprawling park that bears the name of his impish nemesis. Here, kids rule and childish fun and games are the main agenda. There are Dennises everywhere, even some adults who seem to relish some of the whimsical apparatuses almost as much as the kids.

A playground where kids can be menaces.

The father of the cartoon character, Hank Ketcham, lived in nearby Carmel and designed the playground, which opened in Monterey in 1955. The cartoon Dennis was based upon his own mischievous son of the same name. The comic panel debuted in 1951, and ever since the freckle-faced five-year-old has tormented adults, especially Mr. Wilson, with his brand of innocent antics.

Kids can't get into any real trouble here, but they can climb, crawl, and carry on by using a number of apparatuses, including a high-arched sun bridge of orange and yellow perched over a long roller slide, an original Southern Pacific locomotive, and a life-size hedge maze. Other play equipment includes a wobbly wooden suspension bridge, climbing bars, an adventure ship, and colorful tubes to crawl through. One wonders if Dennis would be able to conjure up more devilish fare if he had designed things. You'd think at least a slingshot gallery, for example. For a nostalgic photo opportunity, there's a cypress tree stump carved into the figures of Dennis, his dog Ruff, and friend Margaret.

There is one bummer for kids as they enter the park. It's a Mr. Wilson-like warning sign explaining the dangers of using some of the equipment unless you're really careful. It's as if the crabby-faced neighbor of Dennis the Menace is scolding everyone as they walk in, hoping to undermine their good time.

The playground is located at the city's El Estero Park at the intersection of Camino El Estero and Pearl Street.

A COMMAND PERFORMANCE
Monterey

A New York regiment of bored soldiers founded California's first theater in 1848. Mired in the drudgery of military duty, these thespians with muskets amused each other by performing plays when they weren't performing the work of soldiers. When their military service was up, they turned professional, creating a makeshift theater in Monterey within a building run as a sailors' boarding house.

This theater has a dramatic history.

Jack Swan built the adobe structure in 1846 with money he had made from his fruit pie business, and was doing well using it to rent out rooms to idle sailors. But the soldiers made a dramatic plea and convinced him to let them alter the building's long front hall so that they could use it to stage plays. Broadway it wasn't. The main curtain was just four blankets sewn together. Blankets were also used as backdrops. A change in scenery just meant a different-colored blanket was hung up on stage. Still, the opening performance was a sold-out affair, even with tickets priced steeply at five dollars. The group had a nice run here with musicals, farces, and even Shakespeare, but soon the building reverted back to its primary use as a boarding house. It seemed that California's first theater had experienced its final curtain call, but years later, after a restoration project, the building was reopened in the 1930s by an acting group known as the Troupers of the Gold Coast. They staged musical comedies there until 2000.

The building is now maintained as a historic landmark, part of Monterey State Historic Park, ten buildings in the area of town that once served as California's capital. It's open for tours; call (831) 649-7118.

THE BIG STENCH

Once you didn't need a map to find your way to Monterey. You just followed your nose, if you could stand it, because the scent was pretty bad. The malodorous wafting came from the sardine-processing plants operating here along Cannery Row from the early 1900s until everything suddenly went bust in the 1950s.

The Monterey sardines were a wonder—plentiful and studly, sometimes measuring more than a foot in length. There were more than twenty canneries during the 1930s and 1940s processing sardines at a furious rate. At peak periods the fish came in at a rate of ten tons a minute. Netting one billion sardines per year propelled Monterey to the title of Sardine Capital of the World.

About a third of the sardines ended up in cans for food, but much of the catch was baked dry and ground into by-products such as cooking oil, fertilizer, fish meal, and pig feed. It was this processing that generated the great stink.

While the canneries might have had the sweet smell of success to entrepreneurs, the dreadful aroma of the plants wasn't nearly as lovable for everyone else. Monterey was unfavorably compared with its neighbors Carmel, a town with a scenic coastline, and Pacific Grove, a community founded as a Methodist retreat, with the old expression: "Carmel by the sea, Pacific Grove by God, and Monterey by the smell." That's the stigma that goes along with being the world's reigning sardine kings.

The repellent scent of sardine processing is long gone, as are the sardines, which suddenly disappeared in the 1950s after enduring years of intensive fishing. Today visitors are attracted to Monterey's new Cannery Row, a tourist destination of shops, restaurants, hotels, and the popular Monterey Bay Aquarium, where most of the fish are behind glass, so you can't even smell them.

A Celebration That Creeps Up on People
Morgan Hill

Horror-movie directors have long known that casting a big hairy spider to crawl across someone's body or face is a guaranteed way to conjure up a spine-tingling cinematic moment. These on-screen cameos are just one way big spiders, especially tarantulas, have been demonized through the ages. Long ago it was even believed that spiders caused the plague.

Clearing up misconceptions about tarantulas, North America's largest spiders, is one purpose behind the annual TarantulaFest and Barbecue at Henry W. Coe State Park. Ranger Barry Breckling, an organizer of the event, insists that native tarantulas aren't creepy at all. They're fragile, docile creatures and "it would be hard to get one to bite you," he insists. Still, he knows that getting visitors to view tarantulas as cute and cuddly takes some work. The lighthearted nature of the event helps. People can pose for pictures with the eight-legged spiders crawling over them, or they can go on guided hikes to see them in the wild. There is tarantula-themed food, including bug smoothies, a drink with two straws so that kids can "imitate a tarantula sucking the insides out of a bug," Breckling says. A highlight is a performance by the resident jug band, the Tarantulas.

The timing of the festival coincides with the tarantula's autumn mating cycle, an epic adventure in itself. While tarantulas live underground, when males turn seven they venture from their burrow in search of a mate, risking the hazards of the outside world in their quest to coax a female out in the open for a bit of spider hanky-panky. When it's over, the female returns home to hatch her offspring, while the male is left out in the cold to die during winter.

While visitors may recoil from seeing tarantulas scurrying about on hiking trails in the fall, there's not a lot to fear, Breck-

This spider ain't so itsy-bitsy. Photo: Rosemary Rideout.

ling says. He points out that a spider bite is no worse than a bee sting. Meanwhile, it's the spider that is more at risk, more often than not ending up crunched under a hiker's boot.

You can crawl over to www.coepark.org for more information on the festival.

A ROYAL WELCOME FOR PINT-SIZE VISITORS
Pacific Grove

No one in this coastal community knows how thousands of monarch butterflies magically return each fall. Everyone is just glad they do. Pacific Grove has stacked considerable civic pride—and banked many tourist dollars—on the fact that the butterflies find their way back each October and stay through the winter.

Pacific Grove calls itself Butterfly Town U.S.A, and the title is backed up with laws and action. It's the only town in the country that imposes a $1,000 fine on anyone caught "molesting a butterfly in any way." The town has set aside a 2.4-acre sanctuary of Monterey pines and eucalyptus trees for the monarchs, who seem to relish its amenities, such as the right mix of light and shade, moderate temperatures, moisture, and shelter from the wind. Locals have planted butterfly gardens around the sanctuary to provide ready nectar for the monarchs in an area the town calls a "hospitality zone."

The annual Butterfly Parade, a procession of elementary schoolkids dressed as butterflies, caterpillars, and flowers, is held the first Saturday in October to signal the start of the butterfly season. Visitors begin arriving at the sanctuary to witness the sight of thousands of butterflies clustered in trees, their orange and black wings fluttering. Tourists get to Pacific Grove with maps. How the butterflies know the way is another story. After they leave in February, they will go through at least three more generations during the spring and summer as they disperse through western regions of the United States and Canada before another migration the following October. Scientists have theories but no sure explanation for how these descendants can engineer a

Where monarchs reign.

pinpoint journey of hundreds of miles to a place they've never been. It could be genetic coding, or some guidance from the earth's magnetic field. Or maybe someone in the Pacific Grove Chamber of Commerce sends them all brochures each summer.

Flutter over to the sanctuary on Ridge Road near Lighthouse Avenue. For more information, call Friends of the Monarchs at (831) 375–0982 or visit the group's Web site at www.pgmonarchs .org.

THESE HOLLYWOOD STARS HAVE AN INSTINCT FOR THE JOB
Salinas

Animal stars of the screen, from lions with full manes to less-in-demand oddballs such as porcupines and turtles, can't get by on looks alone. They're trained just like any other actor, maybe even more so than some of their human counterparts. They have to hit their marks and be convincing. A bear mauling on screen has to look real and frightening and not like some staged battle you'd see at a professional wrestling show. More importantly, animal actors must suppress their destructive instincts and refrain from, say, biting a costar or doing something as uncouth as pooping on the set.

At the Wild Things ranch, animal actors aren't born but developed after years of hard training. The company places dozens of animals in films and commercials, from an elephant and giant sloth in *Dr. Dolittle* to a lion in *Donnie Brasco*.

These stars with claws and fur are more accessible than some well-known box office draws with two legs and not four. Wild Things hosts daily facility tours where visitors can meet some of the animal actors up close. You can get even closer if you sign up for some of their special packages that include longer stays and more exposure to the animals. Getting autographs is another story. Wild Things is located at 400 River Road and can be reached at (831) 455–3180.

PUTTING THE FUN IN FUNGUS
Santa Cruz

On some level a fungus is nothing to celebrate, a parasitic, foul-smelling mold that shows up as house mildew or something itchy and gross between your toes. But hey, call it a mushroom and sauté it in a pan with a little garlic and Marsala wine, and you've got a sauce that will make some people salivate. For those folks there is the annual fungophile frenzy here known as the Fungus Fair.

The event began in 1974 and is now one of the nation's largest. It's a weekend of mushroom mania. There are cooking demonstrations, of course, with chefs preparing dishes ranging from mushroom lasagna to mushroom cheesecake, and presentations about medicinal uses for mushrooms (some can lower cholesterol or ease symptoms of bronchitis). You can even learn how to use mushrooms to dye clothes.

Members of the Fungus Federation of Santa Cruz, an event cosponsor along with the city's Museum of National History, prepare for the event by gathering dozens of different types of wild mushrooms growing in the Santa Cruz Mountains. Then they create an indoor forest display that shows how each mushroom grows in the wild, an impressive and artistic centerpiece to the fair.

Up to 4,000 different types of mushrooms thrive in the area's moist climate. As the Fungus Federation slogan goes, "When it rains, it spores." Visitors to the fair bring in mushrooms they've plucked from around town to have them evaluated by a panel of experts. Mostly they want to make sure what they've picked is edible and not something poisonous. Mushrooms are tricky that way.

The Fungus Fair is held every January at the Louden Nelson Center at 301 Center Street. For more information check out the federation's Web site at www.fungusfed.org or call the group's hotline at (831) 684–2275.

No Ups and Downs for This Roller Coaster
Santa Cruz

O ld, creaky, low-tech, and wooden are not terms normally used
to describe one of America's premiere thrill rides. Yet they
apply to the Giant Dipper, the ageless wonder and main attraction
of Santa Cruz's time-warp Boardwalk. Built in 1924 for only
$50,000, the Dipper is a throwback ride that has never tumbled
from grace with coaster enthusiasts, even in an age of rocket-fast
rides with far more electrifying and complex maneuvers than the
Dipper's humble but stirring charms.

The Giant Dipper is the West Coast's oldest roller coaster and a
National Historic Landmark. Former rivals, such as coasters at
Long Beach and Santa Monica, have long since closed, but the
Dipper just keeps clickety-clacking along. Seasonal coats of fresh
white paint on its lattice-wood construction belie its age.

The Dipper was conceived and built by Authur Looff, who said
he envisioned a combination "earthquake, balloon ascension, and
aeroplane drop." Its sleek-nosed cars offer a mere lap-bar
restraint. The ride begins with a whirling dash through a pitch-
black tunnel and then a teasingly slow journey up a 70-foot first
climb along the red-lined track offering scenic views of Monterey
Bay. Then the cars plummet into the first turn, followed by a
series of clever dips where the cars make last-second plunges
before hitting overhead beams. There are several jarring fan
curves where it seems as if riders hover a few inches above their
seats. A few more shrieks and dips and then a jarring halt back
at the start.

While modern coasters race along at twice the Dipper's maximum of 55 mph, none can match the Dipper's enduring appeal.

The thrill isn't gone at this old coaster.

Just stand at its exit and watch as riders emerge, windblown and smiling, car after car.

For another vintage ride at much slower speeds, try the Boardwalk's hand-carved carousel, another landmark built by Authur Looff's father, Charles, in 1911. In fact, the entire Boardwalk—with aromas of fried snacks, saltwater taffy, and suntan lotion, and old-style rides and carnival games—is a well-preserved slice of seaside Americana. Take a ride over to 400 Beach Street or visit online at www.beachboardwalk.com.

How A Sinister Plot was Hatched

*T*housands of deranged seabirds, acting like feathered drunks, terrorize a California coastal community by slamming into homes and pecking away at residents. Sound familiar? Most people would recognize the story line of Alfred Hitchcock's 1963 thriller The Birds. Not as well known is that the movie was inspired by an actual bird frenzy that occurred along the Monterey Bay coast two years before the film's release.

On the night of August 17, 1961, thousands of seabirds invaded the coastal communities of Santa Cruz and Capitola, biting people and crashing into homes and buildings. By morning the streets were littered with bird carcasses. The Santa Cruz Sentinel, which covered the story, reported days later that Hitchcock, who had a home in nearby Scotts Valley, had called requesting a copy of the article. He used this report, and a story by Daphne du Maurier, to craft his chiller, though he set it farther north in Bodego Bay.

Scientists originally thought the birds had become crazed after being confused in the fog. Years later they discovered that a naturally occurring poison found in algae and contained in anchovies the birds had eaten likely caused the rampage.

Hitchcock discovered other ways to transform elements of scenic Monterey Bay into on-screen horror. He used the coastline here to film seaside scenes for his thriller Suspicion. And a former Santa Cruz hotel at 80 Front Street was the basis for the sinister Bates Motel in Psycho. Meanwhile, the Bates mansion was inspired by another Santa Cruz building, a house at the intersection of Broadway and Ocean Streets.

AN ATHLETIC PROGRAM COVERED IN SLIME
Santa Cruz

While most schools prefer an athletic mascot to be somewhat fierce and intimidating, the students at the University of California at Santa Cruz go in a completely different direction. Of course, this is a student body that always marches to the beat of its own pom-pom. By an overwhelming vote in 1986, students chose the banana slug to represent their athletes in battle. That's right, a yellow and spineless snail-like creature. It's a mollusk that doesn't even have a shell.

For years the slug was the school's unofficial mascot, but then the slimy symbol was challenged in 1980. That's when Chancellor Robert Seinscheimer, hoping to update the campus's counterculture image, set out to squish the slug and name a new mascot. He pointed out the obvious weaknesses of the slug to students, including its slimy skin and sluggish nature. Then he did the unthinkable and declared the official school mascot the sea lion. The more dashing image of a sea lion was even painted on the center of the school's basketball court. That's when students showed the grit and competitiveness not often displayed on the school's athletic fields. They vehemently rallied in support of the slug until a chastened Seinscheimer backed down and embraced the slippery creature in 1986, when it became the school's official mascot.

Shouts of "Slime 'em, Slugs!" ring out often at sporting events here, a low-key rallying cry that fits the school's philosophy that "the joy of participating is more important than winning." Images of Sammy the Slug are everywhere on campus, even on student ID cards and official school clothing. The slug has led the school to victory in one major category: It's often the winner of polls to name the nation's funniest team mascot.

GOING HOG WILD FOR VINTAGE MOTORCYCLES
Santa Cruz

There's a place in this town where greasy old spark plugs are admired in the same reverent fashion as others accord Fabergé eggs. It's called the Santa Cruz Harley Davidson Museum. Enter and you feel as if you've landed at a Harley Davidson altar. Visitors are revved up by exhibits of memorabilia, photographs, and, of course, several classic bikes that provide a gushing tribute to almost a hundred years of Harley history.

A 1941 vintage bike at the
Harley Davidson Museum.

Exhibit cases include, yes, decades-old corroded spark plugs under glass and other memorabilia such as a worn leather riding caps and goggles and old and rusted motorcycle license plates.

The museum is housed in the showroom of an active Harley dealership. Modern bikes for sale sit shining and awaiting riders on the showroom floor. Meanwhile, vintage motorcycles are displayed in elevated sections of the room, each one seemingly in pristine and roadworthy condition, although some date to the 1920s. There are bikes displayed from almost every decade in the twentieth century, set against photographs that document the era and the marketing strategy that corresponds to that model.

In the slow lane there's even a girl's bike from 1917 hanging up on a wall. The exhibit explains that this was an early attempt to market the Harley name to children and young adults, although "sales did not meet expectations."

Gear up for a visit at 1148 Soquel Avenue or call (831) 421–9600 for more information.

Apparently, No One Here Has Studied the Laws of Gravity
Santa Cruz

For decades visitors have been drawn to a small area among the redwoods here where a lot of weird stuff appears to happen. Balls roll uphill, trees twist as they grow, and people lean at odd and sharp angles. Some visitors report feeling faint and dizzy after venturing into the heart of this mysterious region, a nausea-inducing wooden shack built at a steep angle into the side of a hill.

A man named Mr. Prather, so mysterious himself he doesn't have a first name, discovered what he called the Mystery Spot in 1939 while surveying the area to build a mountain cabin, or so the story goes. At the center of the spot, compasses didn't work and Mr. Prather felt light-headed. A year later he opened the site as an attraction, and it's been causing vertigo and puzzling visitors ever since.

Mysteries aren't solved at this spot.

Explanations for the unusual happenings here are offered in a
Mystery Spot brochure. One suggests that the area contains the
"highest dielectric biocosmic radiation in the world." Then again,
it may also be because aliens long ago planted special cones in the
ground to be used one day as a guidance system for landing
UFOs. As a guide said recently to a perplexed and queasy tour
group: "There's a lot going on here that we don't understand.
That's why it's called the Mystery Spot, not the Solved Spot."

Tour guides wear official-looking green suits and frequently
pull out hand-held levels to illustrate how the seemingly impossible is possible here, such as how a person appears taller when
standing at one end of a wooden plank, and then shorter when
perched on the other side.

Visitors are warned in rather tongue-in-cheek fashion as they climb the short trail toward the shack that they are approaching the powerful center of the spot's force. Some tourists enter and then exit looking frazzled, while others, especially kids, enjoy spending time inside and hanging off the chin-up bar to demonstrate how bodies seem to lean at sharp angles here, as if pulled by a mysterious force on the hill. All visitors recover their balance just in time to exit through a gift shop to pick up a souvenir. Put the laws of physics to the test at the Mystery Spot at 465 Mystery Spot Road. Call (831) 423–8897 for more information. The spot has an online presence at www.mysteryspot.com.

THE BOARD ROOM
Santa Cruz

The Surfing Museum here is clearly intended as a shrine to the sport, but it does give off some mixed signals. While displays of photos, vintage boards, and other artifacts illustrate surfing's glamorous side, the museum also reveals the sport's more gruesome elements. For example, one exhibit highlights a painful condition known as "surfer's ear."

The museum is housed in the Mark Abbott Memorial Lighthouse, a brick shoebox structure named for a teenager who drowned here in 1965 while surfing. His ashes are stored underneath the building. A centrally located monitor broadcasts horrific wipeouts at some of the world's most dangerous surfing spots. In one sequence a surfer takes a particularly brutal battering from a wave, and then is carried off the beach while grimacing in pain from a separated shoulder. If that's not enough to make you think twice about hanging ten, there's another exhibit on shark attacks that features a surfboard with menacing teeth marks evident on its side, the result of a shark assault on a surfer. Photos in the display show bandaged surfers in hospital

Surfing history won't get wiped out here.

beds recovering from similar attacks.

Despite the dangers, surfing has been big in Santa Cruz for almost a century, dating back to the early 1900s when the father of the sport, Duke Kahanamoku, performed an exhibition here. The museum displays a few of Duke's early wooden plank boards, so much heavier and longer than lightweight modern boards made from shaped polyurethane. The museum details the changing styles in surfing techniques, from early long-boarding to more modern methods of quick turns and cutbacks. Local surfers who didn't want this history to be lost donated many of the artifacts exhibited here, including lots of photos of local surfing clubs of decades past.

The museum is located at Lighthouse Point on West Cliff Drive above a hot surfing spot known as Steamer Lane. If the shark-bitten boards haven't scared you away, you might want to paddle out and try your luck after a museum visit. The museum can be reached at 831–420–6451 or surf over to its Web site at www .santacruzsurfingmuseum.org.

EMBRACING A BIG-TIME LOSER
Stockton

As every baseball fan knows, Mighty Casey wasn't the hero for the Mudville Nine that day. No, in Ernest L. Thayer's 1888 poem "Casey at the Bat," he whiffs, leaving Mudville fans eternally gloomy. Casey's fictional failure is so universally known that the expression "No joy in Mudville" is commonly used to describe any major disappointment.

There is joy in Stockton, however, which for decades has claimed to be the real Mudville of Thayer's work. That Stockton is home to the Casey legend is just part of local lore. "It's widely accepted that this is where it happened," says Jamie Brown, director of sales and marketing for the town's Class A baseball team.

Conveniently, Thayer was silent on the issue of the poem's derivation until near his death, when he wrote that the work had no basis in fact and was loosely based on a high school bully named Casey. By then, however, it was too late in the game to stop Stockton residents from believing that their town and Mudville were one.

They offer as supporting evidence that Stockton was once known as Mudville due to the poor condition of its streets. Also, Thayer attended a California League baseball game there in the spring of 1888, where he would have seen a player named Flynn, the moniker of one of the poem's Mudville Nine. Shortly after he attended the game in Stockton, Thayer wrote the poem and it appeared mostly as filler that year in the *San Francisco Examiner*. It rose in popularity when a New York actor performed it hundreds of times on stage, and it is now one of the most hallowed works about America's pastime.

In 2000 the new owners of Stockton's Class A professional team, the Ports, changed the squad's name to the Mudville Nine to honor the city's ties to the famous poem. Much like in fiction, however, the real life Mudville Nine was cursed. The team was sold in two years and the name changed back to the original Ports.

Baseball in Stockton did have one success that Casey's team did not—in 1888, the year that Thayer's poem was published, the Stockton nine won the California League championship.

THIS BUILDING'S DESIGN REALLY KNOCKS 'EM OVER
Turlock

California has its share of donut shops adorned with oversize donuts and hot dog stands sporting giant wieners. The Central Valley boasts a unique twist to such themed architecture in the form of a construction equipment business housed in an enormous bulldozer. Yes, in this town nothing says earth-moving apparatus sales and rentals better than a monster-size bulldozer 64 feet in length and 30 feet tall.

The mustard-colored bulldozing colossus is certainly a reason to pull over and gawk at the home of the United Equipment Company. Owner Harold Logsdon got the big idea after seeing a giant tractor on an office building during a trip to Japan and commissioned his immense dozer in 1976. It looks real enough, with hydraulic arms, an exhaust pipe, and a sweeping blade in front that measures 38 feet across. There's even a giant pile of rubble in front for it to clear away, if it ever gets moving.

Now Harold's son, Mitchell, runs the business, and he's seen the effect the building's exterior has on people who venture inside. "They're pretty confused when they come in. They don't realize they're inside of what they were seeing on the outside," he says.

Just another day at the office inside a tractor.

You spot an eye-popping giant bulldozer with a front door, and your expectations are raised about what you'll find within such a whimsical structure. But the beauty of this building, and the disappointment to some, is that in the guts of this beast there's a functional two-story office building with 1,700 square feet of space. Inside the giant dozer people sit behind normal-looking desks and perform the mundane tasks of renting and selling heavy construction equipment. To them it's like they go to work each day in any old office building. "It doesn't feel like we're inside of a tractor," Mitchell says.

Until they've entered the building, some confused visitors have even believed that they could rent the giant bulldozer. But it's not going anywhere. You can see for yourself at 600 West Glenwood Avenue.

WHY THE GOOD OLD DAYS WEREN'T ALWAYS SO GOOD
Wilder Ranch State Park

If you need a stark reminder of just how far civilization has come, then a visit to this historical restoration site is in order. Every weekend, volunteers at this former dairy ranch offer flesh-and-bone demonstrations of what coastal rural life was like in the nineteenth century. Here's a hint: lots of chores. Trained docents dress in period costumes and toil away at such archaic tasks as blacksmithing, soap making, hand-scrubbing laundry, and brick making. The strange thing is, they seem to enjoy what they're doing. Take Caroline Miller and Pam Crooks, who spend many weekends here dressed in nineteenth century farmhouse garb, tediously hand-sewing quilts as if modern sewing equipment never happened. They happily chat and stitch all afternoon, while in the kitchen another volunteer bends over a hot 19th century French stove and bakes cinnamon bread.

If visitors are suitably inspired by the time-warp environment, they can try to amuse themselves with several simple toys left out each weekend on the farmhouse lawn that would have been used by kids back in the nineteenth century. You'll need a big imagination. Activities include rolling metal rings with wooden sticks and roping a stationary wooden horse. You can also make bubbles by dipping a stick and rope into a bucket of soapy water—that's if you practice a lot. It's not really much competition for Game Boy.

These living-history demonstrations happen at the historic structures remaining at the site, part of a 4,500-acre park that includes miles of biking, hiking, and horse trails, many with stunning ocean views. Former ranch owners included five generations of the Wilder family beginning in 1885, a family known for innovations both in the field and at home. They used a generator to become the first house in the region with electricity. A tour of

A stitch back in time.

the main farmhouse reveals clever gadgets that would automatically open doors or turn off lights.

A visitor center offers historical exhibits about the farm, including a milk bottle from 1920 and a butter stamp from 1885. Elsewhere you can tour a horse stable, cow barn, and tool shed. While the history lesson is nice, you'll come away with an appreciation for twenty-first-century conveniences after your visit to 1401 Old Coast Road. You can use the modern telephone to call for information at (831) 423–9703.

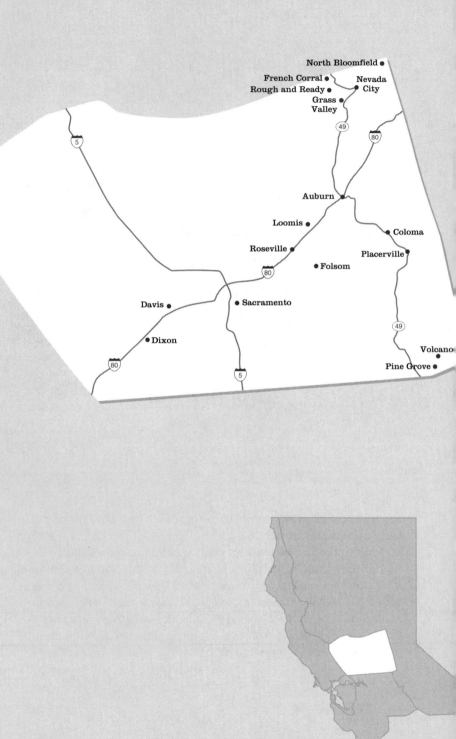

Sacramento Area and Gold Country

WEIGHTY SUBJECTS
Auburn

When it comes to creating art, Ken Fox thinks big. Colossal actually, as in towering cement statues weighing more than a hundred tons and soaring over 40 feet into the air. Fox, a local dentist and self-taught sculptor, displays some of his massive creations in a dirt parking lot outside his dental office building, while others are displayed throughout town. The ones near his office include three figures of Amazon women. One is seen bending back a bow about to fire an arrow, while another kneels with a long harpoon. A third female figure kneels right outside his office door, arms raised in exaltation, as if she just got a good dental checkup. Parked cars nearby provide perspective to the massive scale on which Fox creates, as a passenger vehicle barely comes up to the calf of one of the figures.

Other gigantic works by Fox displayed around Auburn include depictions of a gold miner and a Chinese laborer pushing a wheelbarrow. Surprisingly, no one in town has voiced concerns over the huge scale of his works. A military-themed sculpture, however, engendered political debate. Titled *Why*, this sculpture was created in 1967 and shows a soldier holding a dead comrade. Fox, who served in the Korean War as a dentist, told reporters in 1991 that he made the statue to honor all U.S. military forces. But some Placer County supervisors and local residents view it as an antiwar protest. During the Vietnam and Gulf Wars, some people

*Most dentists just put aquariums
in their office.*

called for its removal from the entrance to the county administration building. Because of strong public support for the statue, it has remained right where it is. Of course moving it would be a logistical nightmare.

Dr. Fox resisted efforts to be interviewed about his statues, preferring to let them speak for themselves. With their immense size, they make a pretty big statement on their own.

A FLASH IN THE PAN
Coloma

Rodney Earle Bland has the authentic look of a hardened miner from California's gold rush era. A bushy white moustache and beard and a dusty black conical hat frame his pinched, creased face. He has a wild-eyed look and a wiry, gaunt physique. His white shirt is torn and threadbare, while his jeans look as if they've been run through a shredding machine.

Part of this is an act, for sure, but a good deal of it is just Rodney, the man they call the Gold Guy. He's known in these parts for his expertise in gold panning. For several months out of the year, he's an attraction at the James Marshall Gold Discovery State Park, a historic site located where gold was first discovered in 1848. At the park Bland sets up a long trough filled with water, rocks, gems, and slivers of gold and teaches the art of panning to greenhorns. He crowds next to them and enthusiastically shows them how to sift through the muck to get to the treasure, while chiding any slackers. "C'mon, you've got work to do," he growls at one young boy who isn't panning with the gusto that Bland expects. As encouragement, Bland pulls two vials from his front pocket, both filled with gold nuggets, generating appreciative aahs from the crowd. Each contains about $600 in gold, he tells them. Still, he's got advice for anyone who wants to make a living out of gold panning. "Don't quit your day job," he says.

Bland has been featured in photo layouts for magazines as a kind of poster boy for Gold Country. When advertisers want to conjure up the image of a rugged pioneer of the West, they use Bland. He's amused by it all, and keeps a scrapbook handy to show visitors his portfolio of work.

Visitors to the park can buy or rent pans and either work with demonstrators such as Bland or take a short hike to the nearby American River and try their luck there. That's where James Marshall first saw the golden flecks that altered California's history on January 24, 1848. The park also has a replica of Sutter's Mill and other historical structures.

The park faithfully marks January 24 each year with Gold Discovery Day festivities. For the more serious-minded, there is a symposium on gold rush–era history. More fun activities include watching volunteers dressed in period costumes demonstrate blacksmithing and gold panning. For more information contact the park office at (530) 622–3470.

THE WORST-KEPT SECRET

*J*ames Marshall wasn't looking for gold, but he found it anyway. Marshall was working to finish a mill he was building with John Sutter when he spotted gold flecks in the American River on January 24, 1848. With hindsight it's easy to chuckle over the decision by Marshall and Sutter to focus not on the gold strike but on getting their little mill project up and running. That's where the real money was, they believed. They tried to keep the gold discovery a secret, but that was hardly a practical idea. A few months later Sutter mentioned the gold to Sam Brannan, who owned a general store at Sutter's Fort. Brannan soon strolled into San Francisco shouting something about gold in them there hills.

Gold fever is hardly adequate to describe what happened next. Brannan's announcement set off the largest mass migration of people in history. Ships that were docked in San Francisco were suddenly emptied. Thousands of people literally dropped everything to become forty-niners seeking their fortune in California. California was mostly wilderness in 1848 with a non-Indian population of about 14,000. In four years the non-Indian population soared to 223,000. With a booming population and newfound wealth, California became a state in 1850. For the next fifty years, miners took out more than 125 million ounces of gold from California's hills.

If it weren't for Marshall's discovery, California might have remained just a pretty place to grow fruits and vegetables. The gold rush helped turn California into an economic powerhouse. The man who started the state's tidal wave of immigration never made his own fortune. James Marshall survived for many years on a state pension, and was buried in Coloma in a grave overlooking his discovery site. Now there's a monument there, the state's first historical landmark.

S*POKES* P*EOPLE*
D*avis*

There are so many bicycles in this town that it may seem as if they grow on trees. Each fall it even looks that way, thanks to an annual student prank that calls for sticking bicycles up in trees and turning them into improbable ornaments that dangle precariously from limbs.

That kind of misuse of bicycles isn't typical for Davis, a university town that claims the title of Bicycle Capital of the World. No other city has stepped up to wave a sprocket wrench in disagreement, not even bicycle-loving places such as Beijing, China.

There are an estimated two bikes for every person in Davis and probably an equal number of bike shops. Davis is an oasis of two-wheeled transportation within a state known for its car culture.

Not your typical bike rack.
Photo: Davis Conference and Visitors Bureau.

Davis was the first U.S. city to designate bike lanes along commuter streets. That happened in the 1960s, when a pro-bike platform could get candidates elected to the City Council. Now there are more than 100 miles of bike paths and trails here, and they're generally crowded, sometimes leading to the unusual sight of bicycle traffic jams. To address the problem, some intersections have special crossing signals dedicated only to bicycles.

For the town's students, a bicycle is as common as a notebook. But bikes are also favored by many locals, due to the town's gentle climate, easy terrain, and the community's overall support of people-powered transportation. The town logo includes a high-wheeler bicycle, an appropriate symbol for a community that has long pushed for pedal power.

WHERE PIGS DANCE AND EGGHEADS RULE
Davis

This town probably leads the nation in whimsical public art. Let's start with the University of California campus, where you'll encounter the egghead sculptures created by longtime art professor Robert Arneson. These acrylic and bronze pieces are oversize oval white heads bearing fanciful facial expressions. One work, entitled *Eye on Mrak: Fatal Laff,* is a two-sided head with one side comprising just an eye that glares out at the Mrak Administration Building. Now that's called keeping a close watch on your chancellor. The other side of the oval head features an upside-down face with a Cheshire-size grin and creased forehead as if the figure is caught midchuckle. It's a popular prop for tourist photographs. Another in Arneson's series features a different egg-shaped face, this one with its nose literally stuck in a book, a great metaphor for student life, at least if you're an egghead.

You should see the playing board.
Photo: Davis Conference and Visitors Bureau.

Throughout the campus and surrounding town there are more than fifty locations where you can view public art, ranging from sculptures to murals. Many works tilt toward the capricious. On Quail Street you'll find *Dominos II,* a concrete depiction of over-size dominos with two of them resting up against a third and a fourth in a teetering position off to the side. There are ceramic dancing pigs on view at the Marketplace Shopping Center at 1411 West Covell Boulevard and a fiberglass rendition of a plump tomato in front of the Davis Food Co-op at 620 G Street.

A map indicating all public art spots and museums in Davis is available at the Davis Conference and Visitors Bureau at 105 E Street.

SAVING THEIR FROGS FROM CROAKING
Davis

If a community's level of compassion can be measured by how well it treats its frogs, then Davis is a city with a huge heart. When residents realized that a freeway overpass was being built smack along a migratory path for local frogs, they sprung into action. With visions of an epidemic of toad roadkill unless something was done, the city approved funding for a $12,000 passageway underneath the new road for exclusive use by their hopping

A town built for toads, if they ever show up.
Photo: Davis Conference and Visitors Bureau.

friends. The Davis Frog Tunnel, along with the town's declaration as a nuclear-free zone, says much about community values here.

Ted Puntillo was so taken with the saga that he wrote and self-published a children's book called *The Toads of Davis*. He also constructed a toad-size village of buildings at the entrance to the tunnel he calls Toad Hollow, which includes a miniature hotel and juice bar. Toad Hollow debuted on the same day as ribbon-cutting ceremonies for the new overpass, and Puntillo's minivillage drew all the media attention away from the gathered bureaucrats and politicos. "It made the officials a little angry," Puntillo says.

You can build a toad tunnel, but that doesn't mean the toads will come. The frogs used to head across the road on their way to a pond, a favorite hangout. But they don't appear to be using their exclusive passageway. "I'll be frank with you—I haven't seen a toad in that tunnel in quite some time," Puntillo observes. "I think when they built that overpass, the toads said, 'Let's get the hell out of here.'"

Showing Mother a Little Respect
Davis

If you've ever wondered how the sixties translates into the new millennium, the answer is this town's annual Whole Earth Festival. Davis, of course, is a town that embraced the free-spirited passions of the love generation of the last century and has never let go. So the town's University of California campus is an appropriate place for a hippie revival, which is partly what the festival is all about. Fashion tilts toward tie-dye, the music and dance are exotic and global, and the food is mostly socially-conscious cuisine, as in lots of vegetarian offerings. About 30,000 people flock here each year to soak up the groovy vibes and to raise their awareness about key social issues, such as alternative energy. Festival-goers can visit booths promoting products such as hemp clothing and solar ovens.

What on Earth is going on at this festival?
Photo: Davis Conference and Visitors Bureau.

Think of the festival as a big outdoor party, but one where everyone recycles. In fact, they're sticklers about preventing trash here. Food vendors offer mostly finger food served on biodegradable napkins. Behind the scenes of all the fun here, organizers seriously monitor how much trash is diverted into recycling bins placed throughout the festival grounds.

Although it was first held in 1969, the festival picked up its theme from the United Nations declaration of Earth Day a year later. Originally it was sponsored by a student organization but now is run as its own nonprofit group. This festival offered out of respect for Mother Earth is appropriately held over Mother's Day weekend each May. For more information surf over to http://wef.ucdavis.edu.

S HEAR J OY
D i x o n

L ocals take great pride in their annual Lambtown festival, which celebrates the region's sheep industry, a major economic force here. The event is not a merry time for local sheep, however, since it pays tribute not so much to lambs but to the *taste of lamb,* according to organizers. The festival offers a variety of lamb dishes from about two-dozen vendors and features lamb cooking demonstrations and a major lamb rib barbecue.

Travelers once stopped here to milk it for
all they were worth.

If that wasn't enough to make lambs feel a bit sheepish, there are also shearing demonstrations and contests. Visitors can watch as skilled shearers hack an entire fleece off a sheep in less than a minute, a feat to marvel at for sure, unless you're the sheep who's suddenly feeling a bit drafty. To add insult to the sheep, spinners and weavers can take their newly removed coats and turn them into human apparel ready to wear in the time it takes to prepare a lamb stew.

An exciting element of the festival is the sheep dog contest, where herding dogs show off their skills as they maneuver through a challenging obstacle course. There are also plenty of fiber crafts for sale and demonstrations on spinning, weaving, and wool dying.

Sheep production has been big here since the 1940s. Before that, Dixon enjoyed a strong reputation as a dairy city and boasted the Timm Certified Dairy, which billed itself as the "world's largest certified dairy" after it was established in 1910. A popular stop in town was the Milk Farm restaurant, which featured a neon sign of a cow jumping over the moon and offered customers "all-you-can-drink" milk for ten cents. Many visitors were up to the stomach-churning challenge and downed glass after glass in a quest for immortality on the restaurant's leader board.

For more information on the Lambtown festival, held each summer, go online to www.lambtown.com or call (707) 678–9615.

A CAPTIVATING DISPLAY
Folsom

Folsom State Prison is the type of correctional facility that gives true meaning to the term *hard time*. It opened in 1880 to house the state's nastiest criminals, who were tossed into cramped and dark stone cells sealed with iron doors. To keep everyone in line, on the first day of every month guards fired off thunderous rounds from a machine gun. Inmates were sometimes

No parole for Sam.

strung up by their thumbs for punishment. Folsom was the
state's death house until 1937, and close to a hundred prisoners
were executed here by hanging.

It's no wonder that residents of this Big House were often des-
perate to escape.

In modern times Folsom Prison, despite its notorious history,
is a major tourist draw. The prison holds about 3,500 inmates,
while thousands of others come voluntarily to visit. Many want to
see the venue where singer Johnny Cash recorded his hugely
popular 1968 release *At Folsom Prison,* which contains the hit
song "Folsom Prison Blues." They pose for snapshots in front of
the prison's massive granite walls and gothic guard tower, rejoic-
ing that they're on the more desirable side of this prison wall.

For a bit of enlightenment about the prison's dark history, visitors can stop by the prison museum run by retired guards.
Exhibits show off some of the prison's sinister past, including
early restraint devices and wooden batons used by the guards to
maintain a fighting edge over the convicts when they engaged
them in hand-to-hand combat. A display case shows off thick
hemp ropes for executions that include an identification tag with
the name of the unfortunate convict it was used to hang.

There is an impressive wall of weapons representing confis-
cated items seized from prisoners over the years, including
knives made out of rusted cans and a spear crafted from rolled
newspapers. There's even a wooden pistol from 1910 that was
used in an escape attempt.

Stop by the cell of perpetual prisoner Sam, a talking man-
nequin outfitted in black-and-white-striped inmate attire and lean-
ing on a narrow cot in a tiny cell. The robotic felon with the
cigarette dangling from his mouth offers a four-minute talk on
prison life and history in a stiff performance that is more comical
than chilling. It's one of the few light moments in a place known
to prisoners as "the end of the world." For information about
hopefully a short stay at the prison museum, call (916) 985–2561,
ext. 4589.

WELL VERSED IN ROBBERY

*T*here were plenty of outlaws during California's gold rush
era, but only one with as much panache as Charles Bolton.
The dapper, witty, and well-mannered Bolton was a respected
San Francisco mining engineer who had the unusual moonlight-
ing job of robbing stagecoaches. The gentleman criminal who
called himself Black Bart robbed more than two-dozen stagecoaches in Northern California. He was ultimately tripped up
in 1883 by his fastidious nature as investigators traced a hand-
kerchief left behind at the scene of his last robbery to the San
Francisco laundry where he was a regular customer.

Bolton's signature style was to ambush stagecoach drivers
while brandishing a shotgun. He was usually outfitted in a
long coat and wearing a flour sack with eyeholes over his head.
He would calmly tell the driver to "throw down the box," indicating the Wells Fargo strongbox, and then he'd be off. Sometimes Bolton would leave a poem behind, which he signed
"Black Bart, Po8." One such offering went: "Let come what will
I'll try it on / My condition can't be worse / And if there's
money in that box / 'Tis munny in my purse!"

Bolton's reputation for being polite stems from one robbery when a panicked rider threw him her purse, and he
kindly returned it, telling her that he only wanted money
from Wells Fargo.

Such exploits made him the darling of the gold rush press
and a popular subject for pulp fiction writers. But he was the
scourge of Wells Fargo. The company's investigator James
Hume finally got a break during a robbery when Bolton fled
in a hurry after being fired upon by a passenger literally riding shotgun on the stage. In his haste, Bolton dropped a hand-
kerchief with the laundry mark "FX07." Hume traced it to a
San Francisco laundry and, in a cinematic moment, was at the
laundry questioning the owner when Bolton walked in. He eventually served four years in San Quentin and was hounded by
reporters upon his release. He announced that he was through
with crime. When a reporter asked him if would write more
poetry, Bolton exhibited his trademark wit by replying, "Didn't
you hear me say that I am through with crime?"

A DISCONNECT WITH HISTORY
French Corral

French Corral is so named because of a Frenchman who settled here to set up a corral for his mules, so you get the feeling that this isn't a town with a lot of imagination. Maybe that's why the residents remaining after the mining boom went bust haven't made much of a big deal about a significant telecommunications milestone that occurred here in 1877. That's when French Corral was the site of the world's first long-distance telephone line. There's a monument here to mark this significant development in technological history, but there aren't many folks around who even know it exists.

You'll find the marker on a hay-strewn lawn next to a driveway with junker cars scattered about. It's a trapezoidal stone with a weathered white rock on top that tells the story of French Corral's great moment in long-distance calling. The marker was set up in 1940, and from the looks of it, neglected ever since. A plaque on the stone enlightens those who can find it with the information that the line was set up here by the Ridge Telephone Company. It connected French Corral with French Lake, 58 miles away, and was operated by the Milton Mining Company.

The line was primitive by modern standards of wireless wizardry. It was strung up on trees and poles and needed a booster operated with a handmade battery consisting of chemicals in six quart jars. The line wasn't used to exchange pleasantries but rather to help the mining company better control its irrigation system for more efficient hydraulic mining. It also served as an advance warning system when federal investigators came snooping around. The phone line was definitely an improvement over another warning system used in nearby Downieville, where workers hung a pair of stuffed overalls on a hotel flagpole to tip off miners of approaching federal inspectors. The long-distance line was used for twenty years. The marker is on Pleasant Valley Road in town, but don't blink or you'll miss it.

GETTING THE SHAFT, AND OTHER
MINING HISTORY
Grass Valley

The Empire Mine Historic Park serves as a stark reality check for anyone caught up in the adventure and romance of the California gold rush. True, the Empire was one of the richest hard-rock mines in California, yielding more than 5.8 million ounces of gold from 1850 through 1956. But through exhibits that include mining equipment and historic structures and photographs, visitors get a window into the decidedly unglamorous side of digging for gold. One picture shows scruffy, hardened miners crammed into side-by-side railcars about to descend into the Empire's main shaft at a heart-stopping rate of 600 feet a second. They're sitting in cars that look like they could be a fun roller coaster, but this was no amusement park ride. The cars plunged the miners as deep as 11,000 feet under the earth, where they spent perilous hours digging through rock in a gritty search for treasured nuggets.

Visitors can peer down the mine's main shaft and get a chilling look at the dark, narrow passageway where miners headed for work each day. The ghostly presence on the grounds of old remains, including railcars, a machine shop, and a furnace room where gold bricks were made, demonstrates how mining was back-breaking manual labor. An exhibit shows how even mules led a harsh existence, with some of them spending their entire lives underground hauling carts of rock along different levels of the mine. In all, the Empire mine had more than 367 miles of tunnels underneath Grass Valley.

The state bought the 784-acre site in 1975 and turned it into a park. Visitors can stroll the grounds and see how the other half lived by touring the Victorian gardens and cottage of the original owner. The mine is at 10791 East Empire Street and can be reached at (530) 273–8522.

HUMBLE PIE
Grass Valley

You can take a bite out of history with a visit to Marshall's Pasties, a tiny lunch counter that specializes in a hardy meat pie favored by this town's Cornish hard-rock miners during the nineteenth century. Pasties made economic and culinary sense as a staple for these hard-working immigrants. They needed a rib-sticking, cheap, hand-held meal to take into the mines, and pasties were a gut-filling solution. There's nothing delicate, or French, about this pastry. Pasties feel like a lead weight in your hand. They were usually stuffed with meat, potatoes, and vegetables, and sometimes anything else edible that happened to be lying around. These miner meat pies survive today at a few bak-

Pie, anyone?

eries in the area around Grass Valley, which has a strong Cornish heritage. At one point, more than three-quarters of the population was of Cornish descent.

At Marshall's, Carrie Locks says her mom, Marie Marshall, opened the store in 1968, relying on a recipe handed down from long ago. Pasties are such an unusual offering that Locks hands out information sheets at the counter explaining what they are and the different varieties available. Most popular is the beef, but they also sell a dessert one stuffed with apple, cinnamon, and raisins.

Behind the counter Locks keeps an antique miner's lunch box that would have been used to take a day's pasties into the mine. It includes a special compartment for hot water so the miner could keep the pasties warm.

Locks was amused when California governor Arnold Schwarzenegger had to eat a pastie when he lost a friendly wager with his Michigan counterpart when the Los Angeles Lakers were beaten by the Detroit Pistons in the NBA Finals in 2004. Pasties are a traditional food in upper Michigan, another region with a strong Cornish heritage, but Schwarzenegger probably had no idea they were also a popular meal in parts of his home state of California.

Each year Grass Valley celebrates a Cornish Christmas that's a big street fair with music, crafts, and food, including, of course, lots of pasties. Marshall's Pasties is located at 203 Mill Street. Call (530) 272–2844.

First in Flight, or Flight of Fancy?
Grass Valley

With better documentation, Lyman Gilmore might be heralded today as the man who made the world's first motorized flight, and the Wright brothers reduced to just a couple of nice guys who ran a bicycle shop. Of course, that all depends on whether Gilmore's claim is true, and that's a very big question considering the lack of evidence and his decidedly eccentric character.

Grass Valley's man in the clouds.

An inventor long fascinated with flight, Gilmore successfully flew a horse-pulled glider in the late 1890s. Gilmore was thrilled. The horse, terrified, bolted. Then on May 15, 1902, Gilmore claimed he flew a steam-powered 32-foot plane for a short flight in Grass Valley. If true, that would put him well ahead of the Wright brothers and their historic twelve-second flight on December 17, 1903. With no credible witness, it was a claim largely ignored, but one that Gilmore made until his death in 1951.

More reliable is an assertion that the aerodrome opened by Gilmore here in 1907 was the nation's first commercial airfield. After World War I the field was the site for staged air shows Gilmore organized.

Two planes built by Gilmore and housed at the strip could have validated his claim of being first in flight, but they were burned along with the entire aerodrome in a 1935 fire. Pictures of one of these planes reveal that Gilmore was ahead of his time in airplane design. It was built with a closed-cabin fuselage and looked much like passenger planes that would come years after his initial model.

Besides his aviation feats, Gilmore is remembered around here for a vow he made never to shave his beard or get a haircut until William Jennings Bryan was elected president. He sported long locks and a flowing beard until his death. The remnants of his airstrip remain today at the site of the Lyman Gilmore School, which boasts a mural documenting the life of this town's aviation hero. The school is located at 10837 Rough and Ready Highway.

Spinning a Bewitching Web of Attraction
Grass Valley

She was born in Ireland and named Eliza Gilbert, but barely out of her teen years she transformed herself into the exotic Spanish dancer Lola Montez. By the time she arrived here during the gold rush, she had already burned through paramours such as the king of Bavaria and composer Franz Liszt. She possessed dazzling looks and cut an alluring figure that men found irresistible. When she settled in Grass Valley, she was mostly known for her scandalous spider dance. The slogan "What Lola wants, Lola gets" is attributed to Montez.

By modern standards, her spider dance seems quite tame. Montez performed it while wearing flesh-colored leggings and an out-

*Lola Montez
stirred things up
in Grass Valley.*

fit covered in tarantulas. Appearing to be surprised by the spiders
on her attire, Montez would attempt to shed them by whirling
about on stage. The gag was that while she engaged in these
frenzied movements, she sometimes dropped key elements of her
clothing, offering hooting male audience members generous
views of her undergarments. What would be considered a laugh-
able striptease routine today shocked audiences in the 1850s,
including gold rush miners who caught her act when she
brought it to California.

Eventually booed off the stage, an undaunted Montez bought a
house here in 1853 and settled down with a husband and pet

bear. She amused herself by lowering community standards with behaviors such as smoking cigars and prancing about in outfits that offered abundant views of her ample bosom.

Today Montez is remembered for her colorful life as well as being a mentor to Lotta Crabtree, who went on to be a storied performer in her own right. The house Montez lived in was reconstructed and is now used as a local visitor center. It's located downtown at 248 Mill Street.

P u r p l e   P a s s i o n
L o o m i s

While long revered in cultures and kitchens around the world, the eggplant just hasn't had many Americans salivating for its taste. The former dish of choice of Chinese emperors, and a centuries-long mainstay in Asian and Italian cooking, the eggplant in America is often a puzzling and overlooked vegetable relegated to the rear of market produce bins.

The town of Loomis has taken a big step toward demystifying this purple vegetable that is sometimes called the garden egg by paying tribute to it with an annual festival. The Loomis Eggplant Festival turns the town into a sea of purple with aromas wafting about of eggplant being prepared in a variety of ways, from grilled to smothered in garlic and fried. There are dozens of food booths offering standard festival fare but also unlikely dishes such as eggplant pizza and eggplant frosted cake.

You'll know it's Eggplant Festival time in Loomis if you spot the event mascot, a real person stuffed into an oversize purple costume, strolling about. Celebrity chefs flock to town to offer demonstrations on preparing eggplant dishes. Professionals and amateurs are challenged to come up with winning recipes in the best eggplant cooking contest. For a more amusing competition geared to kids, the purple plant is raced down a plank in the running of the festival's Egganapolis 500. A classic-car show includes the category of best purple car.

There was nothing special about eggplants in Loomis when the festival began in 1987. While the town has a rich agricultural history, some have suggested that the festival began as a joke, or maybe out of jealousy of all the other California towns and their fruit and vegetable festivals. It doesn't matter now because the October event is a major occasion, and Loomis is full of purple pride because of it. For more information contact the Loomis Basin Chamber of Commerce at (916) 652–7252.

A FEW OF HIS FAVORITE HAUNTS
Nevada City

M ark Lyon remembers being fascinated with ghosts as a kid, so it was an obvious career choice to move into the field of parapsychology. Then he discovered something about himself. "I really wasn't a scientist. What I liked most was telling ghost stories," he says.

Now the actor and writer has found the perfect outlet for his lifelong interest in spirits by organizing weekly summer walking tours of Nevada City's most haunted hangouts. He uncovered the historic gold rush town's ghostly past by going door-to-door and asking occupants if they happened to know if their buildings were haunted. "I would start by saying how I knew this was going to sound silly, but more often than not, people would say, 'How did you know?'" he says.

With its reputation as a rough-and-tumble mining town in the nineteenth century, with dozens of saloons and an active red-light district, Nevada City seems a perfect place for ghosts to reside. "In the early days there were lots of emotional things going on, and high emotionality tends to produce ghosts," Lyon observes.

Soon Lyon had located more than two-dozen haunted hot spots

around town. One building, Firehouse Number One, now used as a historical museum, seems congested with restless spirits. There's one woman who likes to root through cabinets at night, and another "pleasant old lady" who prefers sitting in an upstairs rocking chair, Lyon points out. Then there's a young man who smells like he just came from the barber shop, and a "red-haired floozy" who is often seen pulling back a lace curtain in an upstairs window.

When Lyon is not researching local ghosts, he's writing one-man plays that he often performs during summer theater. The local ghost stories he's heard from others have given him plenty of material to work with as he builds a second career leading ghost tours around town. No reservations are required for Lyon's ninety-minute program. Just show up at the corner of Broad and Nevada Streets during the summer and prepare to be spooked. For more information call (530) 265–6877.

A Destructive Path on the Road to Riches
North Bloomfield

Malakoff Diggins State Historic Park is the site of a former environmental disaster that today is actually a nice place for a picnic or nature walk. The park was once the site of the world's largest hydraulic mining operation during the height of the gold rush. Hydraulic mining was the technical term used to describe a highly destructive method of gold extraction that employed massive, high-pressured water cannons that blasted away hillsides in a frantic search for gold dust embedded in sediment.

Wooden sluices collected the resulting tailings, and once gold was removed, the remaining debris was sent downstream where it clogged rivers and caused flooding in nearby farming towns. Needless to say, the farmers weren't happy. After a long legal bat-

Vintage water cannon once used to blast away the hills here.

tle, hydraulic mining was declared illegal by a federal judge, a ruling hailed today by some as the nation's first environmental protection action.

What remains today here is a massive, man-made canyon more than 7,000 feet long, 3,000 feet wide, and several hundred feet deep. The exposed strata flash many colors and project an eerily beautiful image, especially under moonlight, making this a popular tourist destination. The massive pit is a monument to the greed and fervor of the gold rush period.

Visitors can also tour the ghostly remains of North Bloomfield, a town once named Humbug in 1851 by unlucky miners. Remaining buildings include a church, saloon, and general store. For more information call (530) 265–2740.

HISTORIC RESULTS FROM A DAILY GRIND
Pine Grove

Pockmarked rocks hardly seem a feature you'd build a park around. Yet that's the case at Indian Grinding Rock State Historic Park, where the big draw are limestone outcroppings whose appearance is marred by hundreds of mortar holes.

While not pretty, the cup-shaped depressions are historically significant. They were created over time by Miwok Indians who used the rocks as a sturdy kitchen table. They pounded acorns into the boulders using stone pestles to make a paste that was a mainstay of their diet. Over time you get a unique geologic formation caused by food preparation. For want of a better term, they are called grinding rocks. As an added attraction here, the blemished slabs of stone also feature decorative carvings.

There's more history here than just the flawed rocks. The park contains a re-creation of an authentic Miwok village, including a ceremonial roundhouse, acorn granary, and an Indian game field. The Miwok played a game similar to soccer on a field 110 yards long.

Miwok descendants hold ceremonies known as Big Time events at the park with plenty of dancing, storytelling, games, and Native American crafts and foods. The events are open to the public. If all the cultural displays inspire visitors to get a more hands-on taste of early Miwok life, they can sleep over in one of the park's seven bark tepees. Park officials promise that the experience will be primitive and a great chance to get back to nature. If you forget snacks, you can always try pounding acorns into the rocks. With an aerobic activity like that, who would need an exercise class? For more information contact the park office at (209) 296–7488.

HUNG UP ON HISTORY
Placerville

The naming of gold rush towns often occurred on a whim. A distinctive event, usually of lost riches, or sometimes a feeling about a place led to colorful monikers such as Jackass Hill, Freeze Out, Lost Claim, and Bedbug. Placerville was such a place, earning the sinister sobriquet of Hangtown during the Gold Rush era because of a reputation for meting out swift vigilante justice.

Hanging out in Hangtown.

Placerville residents have kept a tight grip on their Hangtown past. There's a noose on the city seal and local businesses here such as the Hangtown Bakery, Hangtown Brewery, and Hangtown Tattoo. A popular local dish is the Hangtown Fry, a mixture of oysters, eggs, and bacon that traces its first serving to a celebratory meal cooked up for a miner who had just scored a big stake. If you head downtown on the Hangtown Shuttle, you're apt to see a dummy swinging from a mock tree over the awning of the Hangman's Tree Saloon, a bar located in a building supposedly built over the stump of the town's infamous Hanging Tree.

Placerville was originally called Dry Diggins in 1849 because a shortage of water made searching for gold a dusty proposition. That name was quickly amended to Hangtown when three men were tried in the street for murder and then hung on a big oak tree. The name pleased residents because it was an obvious deterrent to crime. Although the name was changed to Placerville in 1854, a strong thread remains here connecting the community to its Hangtown past.

THE LONG DISTANT WORLD OF PHONES
Roseville

In the beginning, phones were technologically challenged clunkers that required strong fingers for strenuous rotary dialing and came in only one color: black. Forget about connecting to the Internet or snapping a photograph with one. A visit to the Roseville Telephone Museum offers a chance to appreciate just how far phones have come, and how quickly, too.

The spacious exhibit hall is probably the largest phone museum in the country. It features hundreds of antique phones and other memorabilia from the history of the telephone, including a reproduction of Alexander Graham Bell's first telephone of 1876 and a working operator switchboard from 1914. There's an assortment of princess phones and novelty devices, including a rotary-dial gumball phone that delivers a gumball with each call.

Visitors can check out hundreds of pieces of sheet music for a variety of phone-themed songs, including a polka dedicated to Bell written in 1877 and more modern numbers. There are antique three-slot pay phones as well as a cutaway diorama of an underground manhole setup with phone cables from the 1950s. The museum also exhibits dozens of historic postcards that feature phones on them.

For more information dial up the phone museum at (916) 786–1621. It's located at 106 Vernon Street.

REBELS WITH A BRIEF CAUSE
Rough and Ready

The mining town of Rough and Ready was barely a year old when residents partially lived up to the community's spunky name and staged one of the country's most short-lived but easily vanquished rebellions. In a somewhat bizarre sequence of events in 1850, towns folk proved they were ready enough to secede from the United States, but in the end weren't rough enough to stick it out.

Three thousand or so residents gathered on April 7, voiced their displeasure with the federal mining tax, and quickly voted to kiss off the United States and instead swear allegiance to the Great Republic of Rough and Ready.

People here were feeling pretty good about themselves until about mid-June, when surrounding towns still part of the United States started gearing up for Independence Day celebrations. Feeling left out of all the fun, the chastened townspeople voted on July 4 to rejoin the union. Local merriment instantly commenced, representing the first time in history a rebellion was put down by the desire to party.

A breakaway republic, for all of two months.

Modern Rough and Ready locals celebrate their town's colorful history with a Secession Days festival that includes music, a parade, and the reading of the town's declaration of independence. Residents dress up in period costumes and stage a musical portrayal of their town's insurgent past. The accent for this entertainment is on humor and not a factual retelling of history. "It's not necessarily accurate," says chamber of commerce secretary Everett Burkard, with decided understatement. There's also a contest to see who is fastest building a fire from flint and demonstrations at the local blacksmith shop, a restored operation that dates to the gold rush era.

The event is a major focal point for the community of about 1,800 residents. Burkard notes that hundreds of other people in surrounding areas also claim to be from the town, proving that it's cool to be able to say you're from Rough and Ready. Call the chamber of commerce for more information at (530) 272–4320.

THE BRIDGES OF NEVADA AND STANISLAUS COUNTIES

*A*lthough they haven't been the setting for a romance novel, as those in Madison County, the covered bridges of California still tell a pretty good story. Two in particular are worth noting. The Knights Ferry Bridge in the Central Valley is the longest covered bridge west of the Mississippi, while the Bridgeport Covered Bridge in Nevada County is the world's longest single-span covered bridge.

The Knights Ferry Bridge is a gold rush relic that dates from 1862, when it operated as a toll road. Fees included a $3.00 charge for the crossing of an elephant. The span is 330 feet long and traverses the Stanislaus River at the town's north end.

The Bridgeport Covered Bridge's main distinction is that it was made with a single span, so it could claim the title of being the "longest single span truss/arch covered bridge in the world," according to a plaque placed near it. Constructed in 1862 with Douglas fir and sugar pine shake shingles, the bridge is 229 feet long and crosses over the south fork of the Yuba River. The bridge was an important toll road for mining operations and provided sure passage over the river for people, animals, and supplies. The bridge was covered not for its aesthetics but because it provided protection for its wooden construction. Today it is closed to all but pedestrians, who can leisurely stroll across it and peer out of windows to get a nice view of the river below. On warm days in these parts, the covered bridge is a nice refuge to seek relief from the hot sun. The bridge can be reached by following signs off Highway 20 just west of Grass Valley.

The Bridgeport Covered Bridge, unabridged.

HOMELESS HEADS OF STATE
Sacramento

Built in the 1970s with state funds, the eight-bedroom gated compound known as La Casa de los Gobernadores was intended, as its name implies, as the official home for the governor. And yet no governor has ever lived there. The first state leader who had the chance, Jerry Brown, sniffed at its opulence and opted instead to flop on a mattress in a very modest downtown apartment. Next in line was Republican George Deukmejian, who wanted to move in but Democratic lawmakers wouldn't let him. The home was eventually put up for auction, and subsequent governors of the state with one of the world's largest economies have been, gasp, renters.

House-hunting for newly elected governors is as much a political tradition here as partisan budget battles. California has lacked an official governor's residence since 1967, making it only one of six states with this dubious distinction.

For many years the state had an official home for its chief, a stately Victorian that was built in 1877 and housed thirteen governors and their families. Then in 1967 the Reagans moved in and then quickly moved out, calling the historic residence a cramped firetrap. They might also have taken issue with the home's reputation for being haunted. It's now a state park and museum located at 1526 H Street in Sacramento. Docents report a cold spot on the staircase there.

While in office Ronald and Nancy Reagan planned an appropriate replacement for the governor's mansion, but it wasn't completed until his term was up. Incoming Zen politico Jerry "Moonbeam" Brown dubbed La Casa de los Gobernadores a Taj Mahal, and not in an admiring way, and refused to move in. The mansion was eventually sold by the state for $1.53 million.

Arnold Schwarzenegger was elected to the office during a historic recall vote in 2003, but before he could tackle the more pressing issue of the state's budget crisis, he had to face the mundane task of finding a place to live. For a while he contemplated commuting to Sacramento from his $11.9 million mansion in the Brentwood section of Los Angeles. Then he moved his family into a hotel. By mid-2004 efforts were underway to build yet another governor's mansion. Schwarzenegger set up a tent at the capitol for an office, under which he conducted most business. That's so he could smoke cigars and comply with an indoor ban on smoking, but it did reinforce the nomadic nature of being a California governor with no official home.

WHEN EXPRESS MAIL MEANT MORE THAN A WEEK
Sacramento

Under a roaring overpass on the outskirts of Old Sacramento stands a bronze statue of a horse and rider who look mighty drained. The gaunt rider, mouth agape as if desperately sucking for air, stares blankly ahead, meekly raising a riding crop. The horse, while making a valiant effort to rise up on its hind legs, looks equally weary, its tongue hanging out.

The inscription under the figures makes it clear why this frazzled pair might be a tad worn out. They represent a tribute to a short-lived but glamorized mail service known as the Pony Express. The Express linked Sacramento with St. Joseph, Missouri, and points in between with a service that employed 121 riders and more than 500 ponies in a frantic chase to deliver mail as quickly as possible. As the monument explains, the service began here on April 4, 1860, with rider Sam Hamilton heading into a blinding rainstorm on the first leg of the 1,966-mile journey. The pouch he carried was delivered to Missouri ten days later. By modern standards of instant text messaging, when even a delay of one or two seconds can seem ridiculously slow, the Pony

These early postal workers were too
tired to be disgruntled.

Express seems laughably inadequate. But it was plenty fast for
its time, and extremely reliable—only one mail pouch was lost in
the nineteen-month history of the Pony Express.

The monument stands at Second and I Streets, very close to the
California State Railroad Museum. That's a fitting proximity,
since it was the completion of the Transcontinental Railroad that
helped finish off the Express. Now horse and rider of this monument stand silently under the steady drone of passing cars,
another transportation development that helped make the horse-
driven mail system obsolete.

THE ROAD SCHOLAR
Sacramento

A funny thing happened to Scott Gordon on his way to creating a parody of a museum—some people started taking him seriously. Well, not everyone, of course, because Gordon thought carefully about developing a museum that would be too "silly and incongruous" to be considered an actual cultural institute, he says. So he opened the world's first and probably only Asphalt Museum. That's right, just bits of road from around the globe, displayed on shelves in his office. Okay, some of it was concrete with cachet, such as pavement from historic Route 66. But the collection, about thirty different pieces of, well, asphalt, was mostly unremarkable.

What happened next, Gordon says, tells a lot about the Internet. He made a Web site for his museum, and that's when the fun started. He started getting e-mails from around the world, with some people making bizarre requests, such as asking him to speak at an international symposium on concrete being held in Milan. "I don't know anything about asphalt, but they were going to treat me as a VIP," Gordon marvels. Through his Web site he brought together a community of asphalt devotees he didn't even know existed. There was an artist who used asphalt as a medium and a writer who created poems about asphalt. Gordon has since given voice to these folks on his Web site. The lesson for him was to be careful about what you parody. "There are people to whom asphalt is their life," Gordon says.

He even got media attention from travel publications and television shows that treated his museum as if it were a viable tourist destination. They went ahead with their stories even when it became clear that his museum was really just an odd collection of pieces of road. "I did nothing to encourage all this. All I did was make up a Web page," Gordon insists. We're not going to stand in the way of all that progress. If you want to tour his museum for real, drop by his office at Cal State Sacramento where he's a computer science teacher. Or visit online at http://ecs.csus.edu /~gordonvs/asphalt/asphalt.html.

WALL OF WATER
Sacramento

At the Sheraton Grand Hotel the mundane task of quenching your thirst turns into an unexpected cultural moment. Climb one flight of stairs from the lobby and you encounter a shiny row of stainless-steel water fountains along a white wall. While most hotel lobbies offer maybe one or two drinking fountains, here are nine—suspended about 3 feet off the ground about a foot apart from each other. The most obvious question is: Why so many? Are people in Sacramento really that thirsty? Such observations make no sense until you begin to view the fountains as found art. They are more about aesthetic than function.

To reinforce this idea, more conventional art in the form of postcard-size color depictions of Old Sacramento, presented in gold frames with expansive white mats, are hung above the fountains, giving the whole wall a museum-type feel.

Go ahead and have a drink if you want, but don't pass up the presentation. Take a moment to ponder the design of the thing before you rush into the more prosaic task of hydration. That's the message here of what has to be the most unusual arrangement of lobby drinking fountains of any hotel in America.

Of course, if all you're after is a sip or two of water, the fountains will not disappoint. They work wonderfully well, with perfect water pressure—not too weak so you have to shove your face

Quench your thirst for art here.

onto the dispenser to get at the goods, and not too strong either so you end up a splashy mess. Just a dependable stream of cool water with the ease of a front push button.

With competition tight for hotel guests in downtown Sacramento, it's clear that the Sheraton Grand has at least one key edge—no one should ever go thirsty or miss a chance for enlightenment. See for yourself at 1230 J Street.

A Place of Grave Importance
Sacramento

This city's old cemetery was pretty dormant for a long time, which is how you'd expect things to be at a graveyard. That all changed in the mid-1980s when a local historical committee decided to pump some life into the weed-strewn cemetery filled with dirt and crumbling headstones of residents long forgotten. Now the old cemetery that dates to Victorian times is one lively place. It's a popular attraction that features unique tours and special historical programs as well as a rose garden that maintains plants dating back to the mid-nineteenth century.

Lectures here are anything but dull and often feature costumed players depicting figures from the city's past. A presentation on Victorian methods of dealing with death featured the re-creation of three types of Victorian funerals and a tour of some Victorian-era gravestones. A program on baseball and beer included a postlecture stroll over to the headstones of baseball players and hops growers buried in the cemetery.

A popular event is the psychic tour, where a local psychic channels spirits buried in the cemetery and then everyone takes a walk to look at their grave markers. There's even an annual New Orleans–style jazz funeral that features an authentic funeral procession followed by a Dixieland jazz concert. It's obvious that things are hopping at this final resting place, located at Tenth and Broadway. For more information, go online at www .oldcitycemetery.com.

THE SHOT NEVER HEARD ROUND
THE WORLD
Volcano

Volcano was far from the main action during the Civil War, but that hasn't diminished local lore about the big role this town played in the final outcome. It's a story about gold and a big cannon known as Old Abe. Memory and historical record are a bit hazy, but the story goes that rebel sympathizers aimed to seize gold being mined in the town and use it to fund the Confederate war effort.

Volcano was producing heaps of gold, and plenty of it was being channeled to the Union side. The loss of this money would have been a big blow to the Union. So "Volcano Blues" sprung into action. Using a hearse as cover, they smuggled a large brass cannon into town to intimidate the rebels. That would be Old Abe. Apparently, all Abe had to do was stand there and look threatening, because the Confederate rebellion in Volcano was squelched without a shot being fired. It's a good thing, too, because reports say that the cannon was so overcharged that it would have exploded had it been discharged.

While witnesses to this historic event are no longer around, Old Abe endures, proudly displayed in a downtown shed. For many years Old Abe was rolled out for civic events and rallies, and sometimes even for crowd control, or so the legend goes. Now Old Abe rests on its laurels, known as the oldest cannon in the United States.

Old Abe isn't Volcano's only mark of distinction. The town has a number of firsts, including being the site of the state's first lending library, a remarkable feat for a gold rush town also known for having three-dozen saloons, a swinging red-light district, and several breweries. With all the excitement, who had time to read a good book? Another first happened on a town knoll where George Madeira built the state's first astronomical laboratory. While stargazing there Madeira discovered the Great Comet of 1861.

Like Old Abe, the town is a mere shell of its glory gold rush days, but it does boast one supreme attraction that draws lots of springtime visitors. That's Daffodil Hill, a six-acre ranch 3 miles north of the town center that features more than a half-million flowers blooming on a hill. The best viewing time is March and April.

NOTHING PRIMITIVE ABOUT THESE CAVES
Volcano

G o ahead. Call Stephen Fairchild a caveman. He won't take it as some kind of negative comment about his manners. He's just a guy who loves his caves. Maybe there's a little bit of bat in him. He left an engineering career in the 1970s to begin assembling what is recognized as the largest private collection of show caves in the country. He's the president of Sierra Nevada Recreation, which owns four caves in Gold Country, including his favorite near Volcano, the Black Chasm Cavern, a National Natural Landmark.

You may think of spelunking as a grimy, grunt-filled excursion through tight spaces and creepy dark places. You can have that experience if you want by taking one of Fairchild's more adventurous and rigorous tours. But he's also developed clean and well-lighted walkways with easy access by stairs for families and those who like their caving on the prim side.

Either way the end result is a view of some spectacular underground scenery, including lots of oddly-shaped hanging crystals. Inside Boyden Cavern, at Kings Canyon National Park, you can sneak up on snoozing bats in the summer or be dazzled by drippings that look like recognizable shapes such as taco shells, Christmas trees, and elephants.

California Cavern in Mountain Ranch, an underground wonderland Fairchild picked up in 1982, is the first cave in the state that was opened for touring, dating back to 1850 when it was known as Mammoth Cave. The current trail includes some of the original paths from when the cavern was first opened for viewing. Some famous feet once walked through here, too, including notables such as Bret Harte, Mark Twain, and John Muir.

For more information crawl over to www.caverntours.com or call (866) 762–2837.

SHASTA CASCADE AND HIGH SIERRA

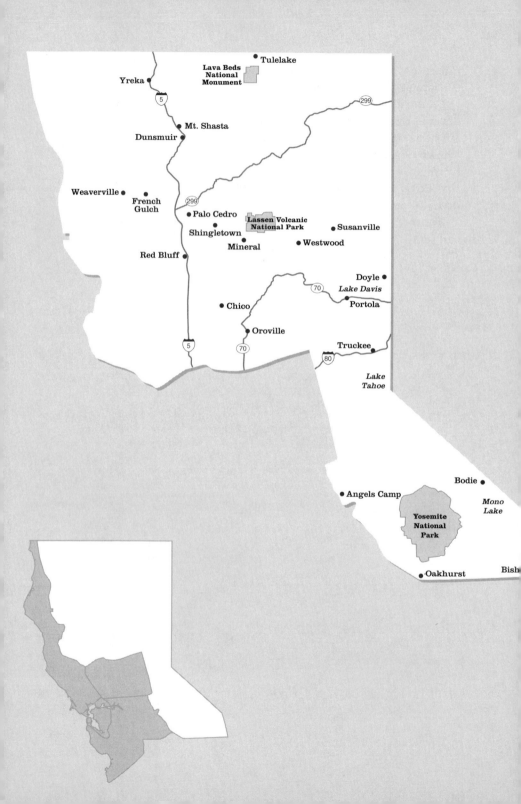

Shasta Cascade and High Sierra

TRUTH IS JUST AS STRANGE AS FICTION
Angels Camp

In 1865 Mark Twain published a story about a frog with prodigious jumping skills entitled "The Celebrated Jumping Frog of Calaveras County." It made Twain a national sensation, even if it didn't exactly glorify the featured frog, Dan'l Webster. In the story the normally spring-legged Dan'l is challenged to a jumping contest and can't even get his belly off the ground because he's been stuffed with "a double handful of shot." So much for fair play.

Twain intended his story as a tall tale. Hopefully he would see the humor in what Calaveras County officials did in 1928, which was to turn Twain's fanciful yarn into a real-life event known as the Jumping Frog Jubilee. The competition is the centerpiece of the Calaveras County Fair, and it's just one way that residents here show how serious they take this frog-jumping business. For example, downtown Angels Camp boasts a Hop of Fame, bronze plaques embedded in the sidewalk that pay tribute to past winners of the contest. Some folks around here speak in reverent tones about the world record holder, Rosie the Ribeter, who leaped 21 feet 5¾ inches in 1986.

All contestants are afforded a great deal of respect. Human handlers of the frogs, for example, are referred to as jockeys, as if they took some active role in how well their frogs jump. Actually, they mostly stand behind them and wildly jump up and

Leaping from a lily launch pad.
Photo: Jeff White.

down, hoping to perhaps frighten their frogs into leaping their maximum distance. If you show up frogless, you can rent a contestant from the Hoppin' Hotel, water tanks that hold dozens of frogs ready to compete.

Thousands of people bound into town each year for the fair, held the third weekend in May. For more information leap over to www.frogtown.org.

HOW MULES GET THEIR KICKS
Bishop

When it comes to saddling up an animal for a ride, horses are the glamorous choice, long celebrated in films, songs, and literature. You never hear the sheriff in a Western, all set to ride out after the bad guys, flash a steely glint at the horizon and declare something like, "Fetch me my mule."

The Packer's Scramble, a wild time at the mule festival.
Photo: Julie Bigham.

But folks in the town of Bishop would say that's just stubborn ignorance. Anything a good horse can do, a mule can do better, they insist. To prove it, the town hosts the annual Memorial Day weekend tribute called Mule Days Celebration.

This is without a doubt the nation's premiere mule festival, with hundreds of mules on hand to compete in more than 150 events, many of which go against stereotypes about these beasts of burden. Think a mule isn't athletic or graceful? You might change your mind after watching them compete in jumping, calf roping, chariot driving, racing, and other skill events. Then there's complete mule mayhem in the popular Packer's Scramble. That's where a dozen mule teams are split up and released into an arena. The first leaders to get their mule team assembled and packed up to ride win the chaotic and dusty event.

Mule packers in the area, who escort visitors into the Eastern Sierra region, started the event in 1969 as a way to open the summer packing season, and the event has grown in stature ever since. Mule Days also features what Bishop officials claim is the nation's longest-running and the world's longest nonmotorized parade. Each float is pulled by, you guessed it, a mule. For more information, check out www.muledays.org.

A GHOSTLY PRESENCE
Bodie

Although it doesn't look like much today, Bodie was once a swinging town. Its heyday wasn't long, from its founding in 1859 through the early 1880s. When things were good in Bodie, they were very good. Fortunes were made quickly here. Miners hauled out almost forty million dollars in gold and silver during the rush, inspiring the once-popular national slogan: "Good-bye God, I'm going to Bodie." It was truly a Wild West town, with daily gunfights, dozens of saloons, plenty of crooks, and a lively

A REALLY
OLD-GROWTH FOREST

*T*hey don't call it the Ancient Bristlecone Pine
Forest for nothing. The bizarre-looking trees are
as old as they come, some having first sprouted well
before the dawn of recorded history. The bristlecone
pines located in the Inyo National Forest east of
Bishop are the oldest living things in the world, with
some approaching 5,000 years of age.

What's their secret? It's not diet and exercise, but
extremely slow growth, as in sometimes an inch in
diameter a year. The dawdling pace of development
helps the tree produce a resinous bark that makes it
highly resistant to decay and disease. Even when it
dies, the tree goes slowly, leaving a single bark strip
that continues to live for hundreds of years while
the rest of the tree dies off.

Scientist Edmund Schulman discovered the
bristlecone forest here in 1953 and then came upon
the world's oldest tree in 1957, a bristlecone pine
named Methuselah, which he then estimated at being
4,723 years old. It's still alive, and now considerably
older, although park officials no longer designate its
location as a safety measure. There are some bristlecone pines here believed to be older than Methuselah,
but their location is also secret.

Park visitors are treated to an eerie moonlike
landscape populated by oddly-shaped trees, contorted from centuries of battle with the harsh elements at this high elevation with variant
temperatures. The trees make do with an average
rainfall of about 12 inches. In their youth the
bristlecones are densely packed with needles and
have a more lush appearance. As they age they
become peculiarly-formed figures with gnarled
limbs, some in tortured spirals skyward and others
on a crooked slide toward earth.

The park is usually only open from May
through October. For recorded information on visiting, call (760) 873-2500.

red-light district. But Bodie also offered the trappings of society, including newspapers, banks, schools, churches, and homes serving a population of close to 10,000.

Things weren't quite so good for the town's founder, William Bodey. After making the initial gold discovery, Bodey died the first winter, freezing to death while on a supply run. Then the town's name was changed from Bodey to Bodie because it was easier to pronounce. The other theory on the name change is that the town's sign painter didn't have enough room to include the bottom half of the small *y*.

Once the mines were tapped out, Bodie pretty much died, although a few stragglers hung in there until a disastrous 1932 fire finished things off, burning down about 90 percent of the town.

Bodie's colorful history is typical of California gold rush towns. But Bodie's modern-day story makes it truly unique among its peers. A state historic park, Bodie is maintained in a natural state of "arrested decay," according to park officials. There are about 200 structures left, and visitors are invited to stroll through the town and contemplate its eerie condition of suspended decomposition. Buildings lean, as if about to topple. Stores still have goods stacked on dusty shelves. There are scribblings on the board in the schoolroom.

What's missing are typical tourist attractions such as themed eateries or souvenir hawkers. The ghost town speaks for itself. Park officials hand out brochures for a self-guided tour, and then visitors are free to roam the deserted streets and peer into buildings and imagine what life was once like here. Photographers love Bodie. In 2002 it was declared the state's official gold rush town. It's open year-round. For more information, call the park office at (760) 647–6445.

THINGS HERE ALWAYS GO UP AND DOWN
Chico

Yes, there really is a yo-yo museum, and its showpiece is a monster toy officially billed as the world's largest wooden yo-yo. It weighs 265 pounds and is a hefty lift at 50 inches in diameter and 31½ inches wide. The only way to play with it is very carefully. "It works," insists Bob Malowney, director of the museum. Yeah, that's if you have a crane. The last time the museum took it out for a spin was in 1996. With an adept crane operator, the giant yo-yo made it up and down about a dozen times. Teaching it to rock the cradle is another story.

The yo-yo's popularity in the United States, much like the toy itself, goes up and down. The spherical string toy was introduced to Americans in the mid-1920s and soon became a craze, but it's spun in and out of the limelight since. The yo-yo gained one stabilizing influence in 1993 with the opening of the National Yo-Yo Museum here. The museum hosts the

Yo!
Photo: Courtesy of the
National Yo-Yo Museum.

nation's premier yo-yo competition, the National Yo-Yo Championship. It also features displays of vintage yo-yos and photographs that detail the toy's evolution, from the first models capable of basic tricks such as walking the dog, to today's high-tech versions with features such as centrifugal clutches, ball bearings, and brake pads.

Public enthusiasm for the yo-yo tends to go in seven-year cycles, according to Malowney. Originally, he points out, the museum was opened as an attraction for baby boomers. "Now we're the museum for the baby boomers' kids, and their grandchildren," he says.

Every so often a new group of kids discovers that yo-yos are cool. Some enthusiasts go on to master yo-yo tricks and enter contests to strut their stuff. The museum's national event crowns several champions in a variety of categories, depending on the type of yo-yo used and the style of tricks performed. The museum is located at 320 Broadway Street. For more information take a spin over to www.nationalyoyo.org.

WHERE LIZARDS RUN SCARED
Doyle

In 1980 the town of Doyle came up with the unconventional idea of raising money for the local 4-H club by holding lizard races. Despite the fact that you're most likely to spot a lizard lounging on a rock rather than racing around a track, the idea actually worked. So much so that the town has built on the event's humble beginnings to create a long-lasting tradition and town party, all centered around the featured event of determining the fastest blue-bellied lizard around.

The first race was held in a square box outside the local saloon, the Buck Inn. Now there's a permanent wooden track in a park. Human handlers enter their hopefully rapid reptiles in individual time trials. The event involves more scampering away in fear

Leaping lizards!
Photo: South Lassen Business and Recreation Association.

than it does running a race. The lizards are placed one by one on a center starting point and then timed for how long it takes them to seek cover and bolt to the side of the circular track.

According to Sandy Eilrich, owner of the Buck Inn and a member of the committee that runs the races, the biggest lizards don't always win.

An amusing sidelight to the lizard races is that the town also holds an election on the same day for honorary mayor, another fund-raising event. People are nominated at a pancake breakfast, and then locals are allowed to buy as many votes as they want to determine a winner. "Our mayor is bought and paid for," Eilrich says proudly, a claim that usually raises eyebrows with political watchdog groups.

The annual lizard races are a daylong celebration that includes a street dance, games and programs for kids, food, and other fun activities. They're held the first weekend in August. For more information contact the Buck Inn at (530) 827–2354.

WHEN NATURE DOESN'T RUN ITS COURSE

*L*ive *government-sponsored sex shows are quite popular in Northern California, especially in the fall. It's a wet and wild time, but it's not quite what you might imagine. The hot action in question here involves fish, specifically salmon and trout. Because of the loss of natural spawning areas for these fish, the state has developed programs to gather them together and help them make whoopee the artificial way. California maintains about two dozen hatcheries, many in the northern mountain regions.*

While most hatcheries are open year-round, the best time to go is in October when the spawning action really heats up. Visitors can watch the breeding process from start to finish and even help out at some hatcheries.

To simulate a natural environment, hatcheries use "ladders" that encourage the fish to swim against an artificial current and into a holding area where they are separated by sex and size. Fertilization of eggs is done by hand, and then the eggs are transferred to incubator trays. When the eggs hatch and grow large enough, they're transferred to ponds to await their release into rivers and lakes around the state.

Come here often?

Photo: Bob Wakefield, California Department of Fish and Game.

At the Mount Shasta Fish Hatchery, at 1 North Old Stage Road in Mt. Shasta, they're old pros at this. It's the oldest hatchery west of the Mississippi, open since 1888. The Iron Gate Fish Hatchery, at 8638 Lakeview Road in Hornbrook, usually holds an open house on the third Saturday of October. A bonus here is that visitors can also check out a nearby creek where thousands of salmon and trout in the wild are doing it the old-fashioned way. For a complete list of California hatcheries, visit the state's Department of Fish and Game's Web site at www.dfg.ca.gov.

MAKE TRACKS FOR THIS MOTEL
Dunsmuir

The caboose may have brought up the rear of the train, but it served an important function. It provided a vantage point from which workers could supervise the train and make sure there were no problems. Better technology made the caboose obsolete, which created the problem of what to do with leftover caboose cars.

This train will not be departing soon.
Photo: Jim Melfy.

The Murphy family in this town came up with the unique solution of turning vintage cabooses into motel rooms. The Caboose Motel, opened in the 1969, features twenty-three cabooses stationed around a kidney-shaped pool. They've all been remodeled to include beds, tables, refrigerators, and bathrooms.

Declaring "I've slept in a caboose" may seem like a dubious boast, but it does have an allure for some. Railroad buffs get a kick out it, especially because these cars came from famous rail lines such as the Southern Pacific, the Santa Fe, and the Great Northern. Some are true relics, dating back as far as 1897.

The Caboose Motel is part of the Railroad Park Resort, which offers more traditional cabins, an RV Park, and a restaurant and lounge made from a converted dining car. Elsewhere visitors will find artifacts related to the glory days of railroading, including vintage signals, a steam-driven logging locomotive, an 1893 Wells Fargo car, and a restored water tank. For more information chug on over to www.rrpark.com.

HIGHBALLS AND HISTORY
French Gulch

If bars could talk, the two drinking establishments in this town would have lots of stories to tell. The E. Franck and Company Saloon has been in the same family since it first opened in 1854. The dark-wooded bar at the French Gulch Hotel dates back to the same period, arriving here from England and brought to town by mule train. Both bars have seen the town through the ups and downs of its early days as a French-Canadian mining outpost to stagecoach stop and its transformation today into a tourist hamlet of about 400 residents.

Carol Jandrall says her husband, Andrew Bouchard, a chef, proposed buying the French Gulch Hotel in 1998, telling her that if she went along, he'd never ask for anything else again. "It's definitely been a labor of love," she says with a laugh. The hotel has eight guest rooms, a Sunday brunch menu, and a donkey named Jack who likes to drink beer but refuses to pull a small cart that Carol bought for him. Apparently, he's one smart ass.

Over at E. Franck and Company, John Felsher is always around to spin tales of the town's past. He runs things here alongside his wife, Barbara, whose family has owned the tavern for more than 150 years. In the early days the tiny rock and mud building was a general merchandise store that also sold booze. Now it's part lounge and museum, with artifacts displayed around the saloon from the town's historical roots, including mining equipment, photos, guns, razors, and even a Prohibition-era still. Felsher says that people often show up in town eager to track down their family history. He obliges by going through the store's dusty trading records to see if a familiar name appears.

Recently the town held an 1850s festival that featured demonstrations such as the reenactment of a stagecoach robbery. But a visit to the town any day of the week is packed with history. For information about French Gulch, visit www.frenchgulch hotel.com.

HE WAS NEVER DOWN IN THIS DUMP
French Gulch

It's certainly challenging to remain upbeat and creative if your job is overseeing the town dump. Somehow, Rob Patterson turned what would have been a depressing occupation for most into creating an inspiring sanctuary and major tourist draw. For several years Patterson ran this town's transfer station. Basically, it's where locals took their trash for disposal. When he first arrived, it only had a few recycling bins and metal dumpsters, but he soon changed all that, constructing a whimsical village and social center completely from discarded items. Call it the ultimate recycling project.

Rob the Dump Guy was king of this trash heap.
Photo: Robert Patterson.

"Even out here in the middle of nowhere, people still throw away too many good things," Patterson said.

He erected a two-story shack with a veranda, a picnic area, a mine shaft facade, and even a gift shop where he offered things for sale that others had tossed aside, including books, old photos, and household items. He also offered a glimpse of rarities such as a deer with vampire fangs and a human foot in a jar.

Locals say Patterson was cheerful about his work, and he merrily embraced the title of Rob the Dump Guy. Publicity about the site drew tourists and so brought wanted attention to the area.

"Can you believe it—bus tours of an old stinky dump!" he marveled. Eventually, Patterson was replaced after a five-year reign as head of the dump, although the company managing the waste-transfer station has vowed to leave his structures in place. Locals are hopeful that what was once garbage never gets trashed again.

A DORMANT VOLCANO THAT WOKE UP
Mineral

B y the dawn of the twentieth century, scientists and residents here believed that the Lassen Peak volcano had long ago finished erupting. Then came an ominous rumbling in May of 1914 that signaled that the long-sleeping giant was stirring back to life. Sure enough, Lassen Peak blew its stack dozens of times during the next seven years, catching geologists and residents by surprise with a series of spectacular volcanic explosions.

Lassen Peak isn't as well known as nearby Mount St. Helens, which drew attention in 1980 with a violent eruption. Most everyone here recalls Lassen Peak's last big spewing period, particularly its activity in 1915. One violent discharge in May of that year sent a noxious cloud of ash and gas more than 30,000 feet into the air, setting off avalanches and boiling mudflows that sent residents scurrying for safety. Ash fell more than 200 miles from the crater.

Lassen Peak is one of the largest lava domes in the world. The area is now the Lassen Volcanic National Park, and it offers visitors the opportunity to see up close the destructive aftermath of more than three million years of volcanic activity. All four types of volcanoes in the world are found in the park, as well as steam vents and boiling pools. Place names reflect the volcanic activity that shaped them, including Chaos Jumbles, an area of fallen rock from the collapse of a volcanic dome, and the Devastated Area, a 3-square-mile area damaged by modern eruptions of Lassen Peak. Other aptly named locales here include Ash Butte,

A peek at the Devastated Area.
Photo: National Park Service.

Devil's Kitchen, Bumpass Hell, Sulphur Works, and Brokeoff Mountain.

Resident Benjamin Loomis made numerous risky treks into the belly of the fiery beast during its explosive period in the early 1900s and took many photographs. The Loomis Museum on the park grounds exhibits many of his works. More importantly for visitors, it's fairly quiet these days.

Scientists are now saying that the eruptions in the early twentieth century were the volcano's last gasp of hot air and lava. Of course, that's what they were saying in 1914, too. For more information call the park office at (530) 595–4444 or visit online at www.nps.gov/lavo.

A METAPHYSICAL MOUNTAIN

Some people come to Mount Shasta to hike, ski, or fish. Others of another ilk come to bang drums, chant, and cavort naked. To some Mount Shasta is a place for spiritual redemption, and to others a great place to catch a nice bass. It's clear that Mount Shasta is a versatile destination.

Mostly, though, Mount Shasta is famous for its reputation as a sacred place among a New Age crowd seeking an inner cosmic boost. Local yellow pages feature an assortment of mystics, psychics, chanters, healers, and, of course, crystal hawkers. It's no wonder that Mount Shasta was a destination of choice for hundreds of celebrants marking the Harmonic Convergence event in 1987, when believers predicted that a special planetary alignment would usher in the dawn of a new age of celestial accord. In local communities such as the town of Mt. Shasta, the Harmonic Convergence is more like a lifestyle than a one-time event.

With so much cosmic energy floating about, it's no surprise that the area has had its share of UFO sightings. Legend has it that an ancient race of telepaths with walnutlike forehead protrusions lives in a secret land somewhere inside the mountain. They're known as Lemurians, and every so often there's a sighting of one, but so far no proof they exist.

A religious group known as the I Am movement has a major presence in the town of Mt. Shasta and each August holds a pageant that reenacts the life of Jesus. The group has a reading room at 600 Mt. Shasta Boulevard if you want more information. If you want to get into the spirit of the place, check out www .shastaspirit.com.

THE BEAR THAT JUST WANTS TO TALK
Oakhurst

Visitors to Yosemite National Park are often warned about the possibility of an encounter with a bear. Those who stop in Oakhurst on their way are destined to meet up with one fierce-looking bear no matter how careful they are. But this bear is a statue, and even though he's got one paw raised in a menacing stance and his mouth is open wide in a growl, this bear shouldn't be feared. It's more kitsch than killer. This bear doesn't prowl around looking for food, and it doesn't even hibernate. It's known simply as the talking bear, and for years it's been offering visitors a five-minute lesson in bear appreciation.

The bear won't talk unless asked to by people who push a button. Then, in a deep bear voice, he offers up a quick lesson on the history of bears in the area. The bear seems to hold a little grudge as he explains how the area of the town used to be bear country until settlers came and took over. Now, this brown bear explains, most bears live in high country and not in town.

The bear is located at the corner of Road 426 and Highway 41 in front of a Century 21 Realty office. Of course, a better mascot here might be a bull and not a bear, since Realtors are usually hoping for a strong economy to keep property sales booming.

A LIVING SPECIMEN
Oroville

Residents in this region were first alerted to the presence of a near-naked and starving man by the sound of barking dogs. Not sure of who or what he was, they locked him up in jail. Eventually anthropologists were alerted and concluded that this was no common criminal but rather the sole surviving member of the Yahi-Yana Indians, a tribal group that once flourished in the Mount Lassen area but had been all but wiped out by disease and massacres by white settlers.

Scientists who befriended him named the man Ishi, the word for man in his native language. Scribes of the day were more crass in their assessment, labeling him in widely circulated newspaper accounts as the "last wild man in North America." Ishi was taken from Oroville by Alfred Kroeber to live at the University of California's anthropology museum in San Francisco, where he became "civilized" and worked as a janitor. He was paid $25 a week to give demonstrations on such Native American arts as arrow and bow making and fire building. Ishi was described as friendly and curious about the strange world he had entered, asking Kroeber many questions while also providing useful information about how he had lived in the wild.

After he died in 1916, Ishi's story faded until decades later, in 1961, when Kroeber's wife, Theodora, published a best-selling account of his life, *Ishi in Two Worlds*. His story made news again in 1999 when it was revealed that against Native American custom his brain had been removed after his death and sent to the Smithsonian in 1917, where it had been kept ever since in a storage facility in Maryland. In 2000 Ishi's brain was finally returned to members of the Redding Rancheria and Pit River tribes, his closest relatives. These two Native American groups united his remains and brought the Ishi story full circle by returning him to the land of his ancestors and giving him a proper ceremonial burial.

THERE'S A MAJOR BUZZ ABOUT THIS COMMUNITY
Palo Cedro

As a professional beekeeper, Glenda Wooten is around swarming hives all day long, a prospect that would make most of us shudder. She endures the occasional stings while wearing minimal protection, not even gloves. The trick, she says, is raising mild-mannered bees and knowing how to handle them "so they don't get all riled up."

As comfortable as she is amid bees, Glenda draws the line at doing the bee beard. That's the eye-catching stunt often performed in public by her husband, Shannon, and cousin, Jackie Park-Burris. They drape hundreds of bees over their faces in a demonstration of the relative safety of handling bees. "I'm not crazy. You really have to keep your cool because they're crawling all over you so much," Glenda says with a laugh.

She's never shied away from bees her whole life, not since her father introduced her and her siblings to his bee-keeping business when she was young. "Some families would go to the movies. We would go to the bee yard," she recalls. Her father, Homer Park, was a pioneer in the bee industry here, and one reason the city is the world's leader in raising queen bees.

Bee-keeping not only gave Glenda a career but also brought her a husband. Years ago Shannon began working at her dad's bee-keeping business, and soon Shannon and Glenda were calling each other honey. The Wootens started their own bee business in 1974 and now maintain about 4,000 hives and sell about 80,000 queen bees each year to other beekeepers for development of hives. Bees are valuable pollinators in the agricultural world, and productive, easily managed queens are in high demand. "Every third bite of food you take is related to bees," Glenda points out.

Bees have often been stung by unflattering public portrayals of them, such as modern tales of invading killer bees. Palo Cedro's annual bee festival is geared to generating a more positive buzz about bees. There are live demonstrations of bee handling, including bee beards, and other useful information presented about bees. There are also crafts, food, and, of course, lots of honey. The festival is held during the second weekend in September. For more information contact the Palo Cedro Chamber of Commerce at (530) 547–4554.

THE DEEP BLUE YONDER

L *ake Tahoe is truly a freak of nature, but a beautiful one at that. Its sheer size, majestic mountain setting, and striking indigo blue appearance make for an awe-inspiring sight. Mark Twain glimpsed the lake and called it "the fairest picture the whole earth affords."*

Lake Tahoe is North America's largest alpine lake, and it is the second-deepest lake in the United States, behind only Crater Lake in Oregon.

Geologic formations eons ago created a large basin. Many streams feed into it, but the Truckee River is its only outlet. That's like turning on dozens of faucets in a tub with only one drain. It's always a challenge to convey in words and images just how much water this lake holds. The most common mental picture offered is that if Lake Tahoe were drained, its water would cover a flat area the size of California at a depth of 14 inches. Put another way, that's enough to supply everyone in the United States with fifty gallons of water per day for five years. Having drained the lake, of course, it would take 700 years to refill it.

Still not convinced what a mammoth lake this is? Consider that the water that daily evaporates from it could satisfy the drinking needs of the city of Los Angeles for five years.

Lake Tahoe is 22 miles long and 12 miles wide. Observers are overwhelmed not only by its massive scale, but by the clarity of its water. Even with encroaching development and pollution, the lake water is almost entirely pure, and visibility is often measured at up to 75 feet.

The lake also provides a valuable public service for gamblers spilling out from the nearby casinos on the Nevada side. A dip in Lake Tohoe's icy waters is a great way to sober up quickly and get a grip on reality after a long losing streak.

THE FISH THAT WOULDN'T DIE
Portola

Almost everyone in these parts agrees that the northern pike has got to go. It's just that the predator fish that locals refer to as the saw-toothed Satan is proving harder to kill off than a horror-movie monster. They've tried electrocution, precision bombing, poisoning, netting, and even the old-fashioned capture-and-kill method, and still the pike lives on. In fact, it seems to thrive and gain strength after each drastic measure employed to finish it off, mocking efforts to drive it out of town.

There's plenty at stake, too. The pike's menacing presence in Lake Davis in the 1990s ignited fears that the fish would escape downstream into the Sacramento–San Joaquin River delta and threaten recreational fishing spots and savage the area's dwindling population of salmon, steelhead, and other endangered species. The pike has powerful jaws and likes to munch on ducks, snakes, and even small animals. It also has a rabbit-like ability to reproduce in great numbers very quickly.

The state Department of Fish and Game took the drastic step in 1997 of dumping 10,000 pounds of poison into the lake as a way of killing off the pike. The move wasn't popular with residents, including Portola's mayor, who chained himself to a buoy in protest. The poisoning killed off much of the region's tourist business and forced the town to abandon the lake as a fresh water supply. And after the $10 million effort, the pike remained, flapping its tail fin in jeering fashion.

Now Fish and Game officials are working with locals to conjure up alternative plans. They've even considered a suggestion to harness lightning in an effort to electrocute the fish. They tried bringing in other predators to eat the pike, including frogs and brown trout, but they didn't show interest in dining on the frisky fish.

Scientists believe that the nonnative pike was introduced to the lake by a homesick angler longing for fishing the way it was back in the Midwest, where pike are common and coexist with other popular game fish. They even believe that the poisoning, in fact, worked but that someone reintroduced the pike after the effort.

For the near future the plan is simply to go after the pike in the decidedly low-tech manner of catching and killing as many as they can.

A BEASTLY BUSINESS
Red Bluff

When Bob Nance first went into the automotive business in the 1960s, he thought a live elephant was just what he needed. He didn't expect the elephant to handle a wrench, just draw curious customers into his auto-repair shop. Turns out, a zoo attraction nearby was closing down and selling animals, so Nance went out and made his pachyderm purchase. "Within an hour they brought over this elephant, and I didn't know what to do with it," he recalls. "It just about killed me the first night. After that, we got along."

Nance later added a Siberian tiger, some monkeys, and several exotic birds. His plan worked perfectly, as people flocked to his Southern California shop to thrill in the novelty of mixing car repair with a zoo visit. But local zoning officials weren't as delighted, ordering the impromptu jungle shut down, a court battle that Nance eventually lost. So he parted with his more exotic creatures and moved his shop north to Red Bluff where he's continued with his theme of autos and animals. He maintains a collection of parrots, lizards, turtles, dogs, and cats in his

*Bob Nance bought his first
elephant to help him sell tires.*
Photo: Bob Nance.

showroom. It's a big attraction in town, and a reason why kids
here sometimes beg their parents to bring the car into the shop
for repairs. "They go home crying because they don't want to
leave. It's helped business a lot," Nance says.

Nance fixes cars and also arranges for kitty adoptions. Dozens
of kittens each year get dropped at Bob's Tire Service, and he
arranges for adoptions right from his showroom. So don't think
that he's all business when it comes to animals. He's had a variety
of pets all his life, starting with rabbits, frogs, and snakes. "I've
always had a love for animals," he says. To drop by for a visit, follow the parrot squawking to 614 Walnut Street.

Bucking a Trend in the Treatment of Wild Horses
Shingletown

The turning point for Dianne Nelson came in 1978 after she helped a U.S. government effort to round up wild horses. The plan, she thought, was for the animals to be auctioned for adoption. Then she found out that eighty of them deemed inappropriate for adoption were scheduled to be killed. So Nelson took the animals and helped create the Wild Horse Sanctuary, a sprawling 2,000-acre refuge for unwanted wild horses and the occasional wild burro. She's been at it for more than a quarter of a century and now has more than 200 horses roaming the lush wilderness in natural bands organized by dominant stallions and their mares.

"Never in a million years could I have dreamt up such a story for my life," she says with amusement. "But I love it. There's a lot of work and worry, but I enjoy what I'm doing."

As a kid she always wanted a horse but never got one. Now she's got plenty of them, although they'll never wear a saddle. They come and go as they please, reflecting the sanctuary's philosophy of offering these wild animals the space to roam freely and live the life they want. "We take the horses that have nowhere else to go," she says. "It's like child orphans. You can't just say you'll take the pretty ones. If they need a home, they need a home."

Only foals born in the sanctuary are rounded up and put up for adoption, usually with great success, since they can be trained from an early age.

There may be more than 40,000 wild horses roaming western wilderness areas, and the government has taken steps to round some up to reduce the population. The plan is always to find homes for them, but because many have spent years in the wild,

Wild horses can't drag her away.
Photo: Katey Barrett Photography.

they can't be tamed. Some end up being killed. The lucky ones are shipped to Dianne, although she's at full capacity now and can only add a few more each year.

The sanctuary is a nonprofit organization. Dianne raises money by offering trail rides and cattle drives for adventurous visitors. You can also sponsor a horse. For more information call (530) 335–2241 or write to P.O. Box 30, Shingletown, CA 96088-0030. The sanctuary's Web site is at www.wildhorsesanctuary.com.

A BASQUE BASH
Susanville

Michelle Zubillaga grew up steeped in Basque traditions even though she lived in California and hundreds of miles from the origins of Basque culture in the Pyrenees region of France and Spain. Many Basque people settled in Susanville and surrounding communities to work in the timber industry, including her family. The Basque language was spoken in her house, and she learned traditional cuisine and dancing as well.

For many years the local Basque heritage was celebrated here, but not the way that Zubillaga and others wanted. The event became known as the Basquo Fiasco because it often featured lots of drinking and rowdy behavior. "Law enforcement had to show up on a regular basis," Zubillaga says. Now with the drinking toned down, the preferred title for the annual event is the Basque Festival, featuring demonstrations and contests centered on the Basque culture. Visitors are likely to hear many warning yells at the event, but shouldn't be alarmed. It's just a contest to see who can do the best version of a traditional Basque warning cry, the *irrintzi,* Zubillaga says. There are also strength contests such as wood chopping and an unusual test of agility and power that requires contestants to roll a granite ball around on their shoulders and head.

In short, it's a family event now, and anything but a fiasco. What's more, there's great food, including traditional barbecued lamb. The event is held the first Saturday in August. For more information contact Zubillaga at (530) 257-7291.

A SOLID SLAMMER
Truckee

This town's old jail escaped the ravages of time to become the state's longest continuously used prison. The stone and steel house confined its first prisoner in September of 1875, a man named William Hart, charged with starting a fight, according to the local historical society. Scuffles, stabbings, and shootouts were common in this rough-and-tumble railroad town with many saloons and a lively red-light district. The jail's two downstairs cells, and a third cell added on a few years later, were usually occupied. Some famous outlaws reluctantly called it home, including Baby Face Nelson, Machine Gun Kelly, and "Ma" Spinelli.

The old bastille locked up its last prisoner in 1964 when it clinked shut for good, at least as a jail. The building was made to last, with 32-inch walls and steel doors weighing 200 pounds each. The structure remains at the corner of Spring and Jabboom Streets and is now a historical museum and also the occasional site of local chamber of commerce mixers. It's open to visitors on weekends from late May through Labor Day. For more information, contact the Truckee-Donner Historical Society at (530) 582–0893.

Another well-known stone structure in town isn't man-made but a freakish construction of nature. It's called the Rocking Stone, and it features a seventeen-ton stone atop a boulder that was said to be so perfectly balanced that it would rock back and forth at the slightest touch. Visitors will have to take the word of historians on that because the rocking stone was cemented in place in 1953 as a safety measure.

During the late 1800s resident C. F. McGlashan built a massive gazebo-like tower over the rocking stone with Roman arches and walls of paneled glass, using the structure to display his promi-

Truckee's famous rocking stone, unfortunately cemented in place.
Photo: Truckee-Donner Historical Society.

nent butterfly collection. The peculiar landmark served as an observation post during World War II for civil defense units keeping a watch over railroad lines below. In 1953 McGlashan's deteriorating tower was torn down and replaced with a replica that stands today on High Street right behind the Old Jail Museum. For more information on this and other Truckee landmarks, visit www.truckee.com.

CELEBRATED FAILURE
Truckee

O f all the wagon trains that headed west during the 1800s, the most famous ended in disaster. Yes, westward expansion sometimes wasn't pretty, and to prove it there's the gruesome tale of the Donner Party. Thousands of people made the arduous trek by wagon from points east seeking their fortunes in California and Oregon. The Donner Party is the name most often associated with this great period of migration, a group whose dream of a better life out west turned into a nightmare of suffering and ultimately cannibalism.

In the spring of 1846, George Donner led a party of eighty-seven men, women, and children from Illinois and headed to California via the Emigrant Trail, a well-traveled route. The moral of their experience might be that sometimes shortcuts don't pay. The group made a fateful decision to try a cutoff and separated from the main group, but their course actually added several precious weeks of traveling time. By the time they arrived at the mountains in California, it was late October, and an early brutal winter had begun, trapping them in Truckee for several months. Weary and starving, many died, and those that survived were forced to eat the flesh of the deceased in order to make it through the harsh winter. In all, forty-seven perished before the group was rescued in the spring.

The Donner Party is well remembered here. There's Donner Lake, Donner Pass, and Donner Memorial State Park. The park features a pioneer statue that shows a bronzed emigrant family scanning the horizon, perhaps looking for a way out of danger, as well as a massive monument 22 feet high, same as the snow level the year the Donner Party became trapped here. There's also an Emigrant Trail Museum on the park grounds that features artifacts from the Donner group. Their ghastly story accents why a survivor, Virginia Reed, later remarked to others making the same journey: "Take no cutoffs and hurry along as fast as you can."

The park can be reached by calling (530) 582–7892.

A Hot Time in Lava Country
Tulelake

Thousands of years ago you wouldn't want to be hanging around this town. Back then, frequent volcanic eruptions that spewed scalding lava and noxious gases made this one inhospitable place. Jump ahead a few geologic eras and this region has become a wonderland of discovery thanks to its violent volcanic past. What was once a lot of hot air and molten rock has now cooled to produce an adventure playground featuring dozens of lava caves.

Lava Beds National Monument is a cave explorer's paradise.
Photo: Cave Research Foundation.

There are more than 500 volcanic caves inside the Lava Beds National Monument, the nation's premiere region for these types of formations. More are being discovered all the time. The unique hideaways were formed thousands of years ago when rivers of hot lava crusted over and formed a hard outer shell, eventually creating rock tubes that are big enough to crawl into and explore. About two dozen of the caves have been developed for safe exploration for families, says park ranger George Freeland. One, the Catacombs, has over a mile of tunnels to explore. Some feature lavacicles, ceiling drippings that have hardened as they cooled. Others, such as the Golden Dome Cave, have tinted walls and ceilings due to a feature unscientifically called lava tube slime. Spelunkers need flashlights, hard headgear, warm clothes, and a bit of courage to venture in these tubes. Visitors may come upon bats and snakes, as well as some tight squeezes. For a creepy cave experience, try Skull Ice Cave, which gets its name for the many sheep skulls littered throughout.

There are plenty of treasures aboveground in the park, too, including cinder cones, which are lava formations that cooled in the air, and many other intricately shaped volcanic ruins.

A group of fifty-three Modoc Indians used the shelter of the lava beds to hide from and attack U.S. Army soldiers who came for them in 1873 for removal to a reservation. The small band held out against greater numbers for more than five months before they were captured. Visitors can see some Native American pictographs that survive today on cave walls. For more information call the park headquarters at (530) 667–2282 or explore the park's Web site at www.nps.gov/labe.

DISPENSING A STRONG DOSE OF HISTORY
Weaverville

Patricia and Frank Hicks Jr. take pride in keeping their business stuck in the past. Modernization? Forget about it. Not here. "We work hard to keep the store old," says Patricia, not normally a happy declaration by entrepreneurs who want to stay in business. But for Patricia and Frank Jr., it all makes sense. They are the owners of the oldest drugstore in California and possibly, Patricia believes, west of the Mississippi. They bought the Weaverville Drug Store in 1967 from Frank's family, which had owned it since 1941. The store first opened in 1852, two years after the town was founded, and it's been there ever since, dispensing a variety of ointments, pills, and assorted medications for generations of afflicted locals and visitors.

The store, in fact, is like a pharmaceutical museum, filled with all sorts of antique fixtures and medical equipment that draw hundreds of curious visitors a year along with others just needing some medical help. Over the front door there are apothecary jars from the 1850s. Elsewhere there are antique pill-rolling machines, mortar and pestles, and even leech jars from the days when bloodletting was standard medical practice.

Nowadays you can get more-modern medical aid at the store. And you can also satisfy your sweet tooth here pretty cheaply. Another thing that hasn't changed here is penny candy—it still costs a penny. The Hickses buy about 800 pounds of it at a time to stock up.

"It's such a neat place. It has atmosphere," Patricia says. How many other drugstores can you say that about? See for yourself at 219 Main Street. Call (530) 623–4343 for more information.

S P I R I T S   F O R   T H E   S P I R I T   G O D S
Weaverville

Alcohol and religious services usually don't mix, except at this town's historic Joss House, the oldest continuously-used Chinese temple in California. In keeping with its Taoist traditions, the temple features altars where worshippers can make offerings of food and liquor to several gods, bribes given to curry favor from these deities. It's not unusual for visitors to find bottles of Scotch or other alcoholic tributes placed on the wooden offering tables, in addition to food and incense candles.

That's how the faithful have prayed here since 1853, when the local Chinese community constructed their first temple in Weaverville. The Chinese were drawn to this remote California region by the area's gold rush in the mid-1800s. Although the original house of worship burned down in 1873, a replacement went up a year later, showing the importance of having this religious and social center for a population that was far from home and their native traditions. Residents named it the Temple of the Forest Beneath the Clouds. It became a state park in 1956, thanks to the efforts of local grocer Moon Lee.

Weaverville's Joss House is so authentic that visitors come from China to see what a nineteenth century Chinese Taoist temple looked like. The temple is still used as a place of worship and is closed to visitors when followers are here to pray. But it's also a destination for those interested in Chinese history. The shrine reveals much about what life was like for immigrant Chinese in the rugged mining camps of the nineteenth century. Mining tools are displayed, along with weapons used in an 1854 tong war. Altars are set up to receive offerings from gods responsible for health, fortune, and travel, areas of great concern to the immigrant population who made an arduous journey here seeking riches in the area's gold region. The temple's wooden doors are considered spirit screens to ward off evil forces.

For more information phone the visitor center at (530) 623–5284. The park is located at the southwest corner of Highway 299 and Oregon Street.

He's a Lumberjack and More Than Just OK
Westwood

When William Laughead was asked to come up with an advertising campaign for the Red River Lumber Company in the early 1900s, legend has it that he drew upon tall stories he had heard while working in logging camps in the late nineteenth century. He put all those mythical stories to work in the character of a giant lumberman and his blue ox, Babe, creating Paul Bunyan, one of America's great folk heroes. Red River established Westwood in 1913 as a company town devoted to the timber industry. A year later the first Bunyan stories were used in advertising pamphlets designed to promote the company and its products.

Paul Bunyan looms large in this town.
Photo: Westwood Chamber of Commerce.

The Red River Lumber Company closed up shop in the 1950s, but the town hasn't forgotten its oversize hero. There's a 25-foot statue of Bunyan and Babe on Third Street in town, and each year Westwood hosts the Paul Bunyan Festival. While the festival features some events that you might expect, such as logging demonstrations and a parade, it also offers something called Blue Ox bingo. That's where a giant Bingo board is marked out on a lawn, and people purchase tickets corresponding to each square. That's when the fun begins. A giant bull is then brought in and set loose on the board. Wherever the bull's first droppings go, the owner of that bingo square wins the pot, which gets up to $1,200.

Sounds like an event worthy of a Paul Bunyan tale. For more information call the Westwood Chamber at (530) 256–2456. The festival is held every Fourth of July weekend.

WHY CLIMB THIS MOUNTAIN?
BECAUSE IT'S SHEER
Yosemite National Park

This great park, filled with many natural wonders that induce appreciative sighs and awed stares, features many majestic monuments. There's the park's trademark sight, Half Dome, for example, as well as Yosemite Falls, at 2,425 feet the tallest waterfall in North America.

Then there's El Capitan, a name of respect given for good reason to this massive slab of rock, noted for being the world's largest chunk of exposed granite and also the tallest unbroken cliff on the planet. You could just sit back and admire it, of course. But some athletic and adventurous types view El Capitan as a supreme challenge, begging to be climbed. Yosemite is often credited with being the place where the modern sport of rock climbing originated, mostly because of tricky ascents such as the trek up the face of El

A face a rock climber could love.

Photo: Courtesy of DNC Parks and Resorts at Yosemite.

Capitan. This granite cliff is the premiere rock-climbing site in the world, the Everest of the rock climbing set.

It used to take several days to clamber up El Capitan's nearly 3,600-foot ascent, says park officer Scott Gediman. Now some climbers can do it in a few hours. There are nearly twenty routes marked out to the top, he says, but some climbers prefer to go their own way, which Gediman thinks is a little crazy.

The rock was named in 1851 by American explorers. Its original Indian name meant Rock Chief, Gediman says.

While many of Yosemite's milestones and assets are widely known, Gediman says Yosemite rangers have a friendly rivalry with officials at another great American treasure, Yellowstone National Park. While Yellowstone is credited with being the first national park, created in 1872, Gediman says that some of the land that became part of Yosemite National Park in 1890 was actually set aside as protected wilderness by President Abraham Lincoln in 1864, the first time anything like that had been done at the federal level. That would make Yosemite the nation's first national park, Gediman says, although the folks at Yellowstone would politely disagree.

THE ALMOST FORTY-NINTH STATE
Yreka

Alaska became America's forty-ninth state, but had circumstances been different, that distinction might have gone to a rebellious-minded region of several counties in Northern California and Southern Oregon in 1941. That's when several residents here launched what was partly a publicity stunt but also a serious move to statehood motivated by frustration with a lack of public funding to improve area roads. Several representatives formed an alliance in late November to announce that they were in "patriotic rebellion against the states of California and Oregon." A newspaper ran a state-naming contest, and Jefferson won out over other suggestions such as Discontent and Bonanza. Jefferson soon had a state seal consisting of a gold pan containing two x's, representing how residents felt double-crossed by governments in Sacramento and Salem.

In late November several rifle-bearing residents of the newly-declared state staged a headline-grabbing publicity ploy by barricading a major highway just outside Yreka, the tiny city declared Jefferson's capital. They handed out proclamations of independence that stated that the region planned to secede every Thursday until their demands for better roads were met.

On December 4 Judge John Childs was elected governor of Jefferson during a feisty celebration and inauguration ceremony, an event covered by newsreel programs scheduled to air nationally on December 8. Momentum for Jefferson's official declaration of statehood was clearly picking up. But three days later Pearl Harbor was bombed, and Jefferson was pushed from the front pages. New roads were built to aid the war effort, and the Jefferson statehood movement died out.

Today there still are people who proclaim that Jefferson is really another state, and not just a state of mind. Visitors are apt to spot roadside signs painted on the sides of barns declaring the state of Jefferson. State of Jefferson T-shirts and coffee mugs are popular souvenir items in the region. Jefferson lives on, if only in the hearts of its ardent followers.

index

About the Author

S aul Rubin is a veteran California journalist who has covered everything from major disasters to stories highlighting the state's quirky inhabitants and culture. He has written for the *Los Angeles Times* and Copley News Service and was also a staff writer for a national sports magazine show on Fox Sports Net. In 2004 he published *Southern California Curiosities* with The Globe Pequot Press.

In addition to writing books and the occasional freelance article, Saul teaches journalism at Santa Monica College and lives in the Los Angeles area. Whatever he does to make a living, Saul knows that his real job is keeping his wife and daughter happy.